THE FLIPPE

MW00440053

flipped learning for Elementary INSTRUCTION

JONATHAN BERGMANN
AARON SAMS

International Society for Technology in Education
EUGENE, OREGON • ARLINGTON, VIRGINIA

The Flipped Learning Series
Flipped Learning for Elementary Instruction
Jonathan Bergmann and Aaron Sams

© 2016 International Society for Technology in Education

Editor: *Paul Wurster*
Associate Editor: *Emily Reed*
Production Manager: *Christine Longmuir*
Copy Editor: *Kristin Landon*
Proofreader: *Ann Skaugset*
Cover Design: *Brianne Beigh*
Book Design and Production: *Kim McGovern*

First Edition
ISBN: 978-1-56484-363-0 (paperback)
ISBN: E-book available

Printed in the United States of America

ISTE® is a registered trademark of the International Society for Technology in Education.

About ISTE

The International Society for Technology in Education (ISTE) is the premier nonprofit organization serving educators and education leaders committed to empowering connected learners in a connected world. ISTE serves more than 100,000 education stakeholders throughout the world.

ISTE's innovative offerings include the ISTE Conference & Expo, one of the biggest, most comprehensive ed tech events in the world—as well as the widely adopted ISTE Standards for learning, teaching and leading in the digital age and a robust suite of professional learning resources, including webinars, online courses, consulting services for schools and districts, books, and peer-reviewed journals and publications. Visit iste.org to learn more.

Also by Jonathan Bergmann and Aaron Sams

Flipped Learning: Gateway to Student Engagement

Flip Your Classroom: Reach Every Student in Every Class Every Day

Flip Your Classroom—The Workbook: Making Flipped Learning Work for You

About the Authors

Jon Bergmann is a teacher who used to love being the center of the classroom. But he gave it up when he saw how engaged his students became in the learning process when he began flipping his instruction. Flipped learning allowed him to know his students better, which brought him back to the reason he became a teacher in the first place. He is considered one of the pioneers of flipped learning and now shares his passion for learner-centered classrooms with educators around the globe. Jon is currently writing, speaking, and sharing with educators about flipped learning. He received the Presidential Award for Excellence in Math and Science Teaching in 2002 and was named a semifinalist for Colorado Teacher of the Year in 2010. Jon serves on the advisory board of TED Education and hosts "The Flip Side," a radio show that tells the stories of flipped educators. In addition, he is a founding board member and the treasurer of the Flipped Learning Network, the only not-for-profit organization run by and for flipped educators. Find out more about him at JonBergmann.com

Aaron Sams has been an educator since 2000. He is managing director of FlippedClass.com, is co-founder of The Flipped Learning Network, and is an adjunct professor at Saint Vincent College. He was awarded the 2009 Presidential Award for Excellence in Math and Science Teaching and was a chemistry teacher in Woodland Park, CO, and in Hacienda Heights, CA. Aaron also served as co-chair of the Colorado State Science Standards Revision Committee and serves as an advisor to TED-Ed. Aaron co-authored *Flip Your Classroom: Reach Every Student in Every Class Every Day* and *Flipped Learning: Gateway to Student Engagement.* He frequently speaks and conducts workshops on educational uses of screencasts and the flipped classroom concept. He advocates for inquiry-based and student-centered learning environments in which students are encouraged to demonstrate their understanding in ways that are meaningful to them. With experience in public, private, and home schools, in face-to-face, online, and blended learning environments, Aaron brings a unique educational perspective to any audience. He is a lifelong learner, reader, maker, and explorer. He holds a BS in Biochemistry and an MAEd, both from Biola University.

Contents

Contents

Preface

As the first days of school began in 2006, we—Aaron Sams and Jonathan Bergmann—arrived to teach science at Woodland Park High School in Woodland Park, Colorado. Jon came from the Denver metropolitan area and settled into room 313, and Aaron came from the greater Los Angeles area to occupy room 314.

We had both taught chemistry at our previous schools, Jon for 18 years and Aaron for 6 years. Because we represented the entire chemistry team, we decided to work together to develop a strong chemistry program at Woodland Park.

During the school year, we taught in a traditional manner, using a great deal of direct instruction in an engaging lecture style. We also met on a regular basis to reflect about best practices and how to integrate technology into our classes. These voluntary meetings grew out of the fact that we worked well together and realized that two heads were better than one.

In the spring of 2007, Aaron showed Jon an article that reviewed a computer program that recorded PowerPoint lectures, including digital ink that could be written on the screen and audio recording. At this point, we were ready to dive into the world of teacher-created video.

We first used screen-recording software to capture live lectures. Once we started, the assistant superintendent in charge of curriculum and instruction in our school district took note and visited our classrooms. Her daughter was attending a university, and one of her daughter's professors was recording the audio of his lectures. She told us that her daughter loved this model because she didn't have to go to class anymore. Later that week, during lunch, a conversation about that interaction ensued. What is the value of class time if a student can access all the content while not attending class? Why do students *really* need a teacher physically present?

In that conversation Aaron asked Jon, "What if we stopped lecturing in class and prerecorded all of our lessons, and students could do in class the stuff that they used to do at home?" Jon said, "OK, let's do it!" Since then, neither of us has used direct instruction as a whole-group, in-class teaching method.

During this time of development, we shared online with a group of teachers what we were doing. These teachers had been active on the AP Chemistry listserv for many years, using that platform to connect and learn from other AP Chemistry teachers from around the world. As the concept of the flipped classroom grew, this group became a place to share and learn, serving as a sounding board to us. As such, the flipped classroom was not born in a vacuum. It did not develop in rooms 313 and 314 alone.

There are now many communities of practice around the world for teachers who are implementing the flipped class. We, along with Dr. Jerry Overmeyer, at the University of Northern Colorado, oversee one community at flippedclassroom.org, which has more than 25,000 members. Though we get much of the credit for the flipped classroom, it would never have happened without the broader network of other amazing teachers.

The idea of the flipped classroom is really quite simple. Direct instruction is done through video, or some other digital learning object, which students can use individually before they come to class. This time shift allows the teacher to use class time for work that is either better done as a large group or requires individualized attention by the teacher. That's it! The flipped class, in brief, is direct instruction delivered to the individual outside of class so that there is more strategic use of in-class time for group work and individualized attention. We soon found out that we had stumbled onto something that could radically transform our classrooms into something we never could have anticipated.

We have chronicled much of this in our previous books, *Flip Your Classroom: Reach Every Student in Every Class Every Day* (Bergmann & Sams, 2012) and *Flipped Learning: Gateway to Student Engagement* (Bergmann & Sams, 2014). Since the publication of those two books, teachers have been asking us for very specific resources on how to flip different subjects and grade levels. This book, part of a series of books designed to meet that demand, is a practical guide for elementary school teachers interested in flipping their classrooms.

This book serves as a guide for teachers who are beginning to flip their classes, or are interested in exploring the flipped model for the first time. It helps real elementary teachers deal with the realities of teaching in an increasingly interconnected and digital world. Each chapter explores practical ways to bring flipped learning into the elementary classroom, including:

- How to flip your class, and the four hurdles to flipping (thinking, technology, time, and training).

- How your approach to planning changes as you implement flipped learning.

- How flipping will enhance the classroom experience for students.

- What tech tools are available for elementary school teachers to flip their classes.

- How to teach different subjects in the flipped elementary classroom.

- How elementary teachers can give students more ownership and choice in their learning.

- How flipped learning can help with differentiation and individualized instruction.

- How flipped learning can provide an environment where projects can be done more often and with more fidelity.

- How to use gamification to flip the elementary class.

- How to implement the flipped-mastery model in an elementary classroom.

We begin with a story about a teacher whose career and classroom were transformed by flipping.

Chapter 1

why you should flip your class

FLIPPED LEARNING has a deep impact on the professional lives of teachers, but more importantly, Flipped learning positively affects the lives of students. Such is the case for Matt Burns, a fifth grade teacher in Australia. Two years ago, Matt wondered how he could leverage the power of technology to improve his teaching, including the technological devices his students brought to school, as well as the vast resources available on the internet. He realized that if he could record his lessons, his students could access them at their own pace and convenience. After sharing this with his supervisor, Matt was introduced to our book, *Flip Your Classroom,* which he eagerly consumed in two hours.

With these new ideas he turned his attention to his own teaching. After discovering his classroom was equipped with a screencasting device on his interactive whiteboard, Matt created a few math screencasts for his students, also incorporating videos others had created. He showed his students how to access the math videos, and sent slips of paper home with them instructing them which videos to watch each night.

Although his efforts were proving successful, his principal pushed Matt to further explore flipping his classes. Matt started to differentiate his math instruction based on a pretest by directing students to the appropriate videos based on their unique math abilities. Over time, he also started flipping his science, English, and history classes, and has incorporated more advanced flipping strategies, like In-Flip, project-based learning (PBL), and flipped-mastery (all concepts described in later chapters). Matt has continued to create flipped videos and now has a 130-video repository at his disposal. These days Matt flips everything he can, claiming he could never go back to conventional ways of teaching.

Matt's students are earning better grades as a result of the flipped classes. They are also growing socially with the increase in classroom discussion and opportunities to meet individually with him. His school's administrators recognized this success and asked Matt to present his flipped class methods to his peers throughout the entire school district. Two high school math teachers jumped on board right away. The elementary school teachers were slower to respond initially, but over time, he has seen increasing number of them starting to flip their classes.

This year, Matt has been assigned to be a K–12 flipped trainer in his district, explaining the benefits of flipping and teaching others how to do it. Matt believes the fear of losing control of the classroom is the primary reason teachers choose not to flip their classes. We understand this fear, but hope the teacher stories we share in this book will alleviate any fears you might have.

Flipped Class 101

Simplicity is the ultimate sophistication.
—LEONARDO DA VINCI

Sometimes the simplest ideas are the most profound. Think back to BlackBerry phones, with their many buttons. Everybody wanted one until Steve Jobs, of

Apple, told his design team to create a phone with *one* button. As they say, the rest is history. The flipped class technique is a simple idea at its core, based on these two steps:

- Move the direct instruction (often called the lecture) away from the group space. This usually means that students watch and interact with an instructional video (flipped video) prior to coming to class.

- Engage in various types of activities that allow students to practice learned concepts and use higher-order thinking.

We call this basic time shift Flipped Class 101, which reflects what people popularly refer to as a flipped classroom. Flip the homework with the direct instruction, and you have a flipped class. This simple time shift has significant benefits, like the following:

- In a typical classroom, students often go home with difficult homework. They do this work independently and have little or no help. Some are successful, but many are not. In a flipped class, students do the difficult tasks in the classroom, in the presence of an expert, the teacher.

- Because the presentation of content is removed from class time, there is more time for teachers to interact and help students.

- Students can pause and rewind a video. In a traditional lecture class, students cannot pause their teacher.

There are many other benefits, which we have described in our previous books. In recognition of those benefits, the focus of this book is to give elementary teachers practical strategies to help them reach students using the flipped model.

The One Question

Another way to think about the simplicity of the flipped classroom model is to boil it down to one simple question: *What is the best use of your face-to-face class time?* Is the best use of this valuable time with students the dissemination of information, or is it something else? In a flipped classroom setting, the direct instruction is offloaded to the individual space, and the class time is used for something else.

The flipped classroom also helps the teacher deliver content consistently, and to all students. As you know, this can be a challenge in the elementary classroom, as students are frequently pulled out of class for a variety of reasons. With students leaving class for individual education programs, band, orchestra, individual assistance, or many other reasons, there can be times when only a few students remain in class. Shifting the delivery of the lesson's content helps protect against students missing important information, and saves the teacher time in helping those students catch up.

When we flipped our classes our students performed significantly better on our unit exams, enabling us to do 50% more hands-on activities (Bergmann & Sams, 2012). What started as an experiment to help meet the needs of our students became a new technique that radically changed our classrooms, and the classrooms of many other teachers.

Given that we experienced success with this model, you would expect that we would have continued to use it. However, after the first year of the flipped class we didn't simply repeat the previous year—we reinvented our class again, adding mastery learning to our repertoire. Based on the work of Benjamin Bloom (Bloom, 1968), the flipped-mastery model is an asynchronous approach in which students demonstrate mastery of content before moving on to new topics. Each student moves at a flexible pace, which allows advanced students to get the challenges they need and provides extra support for struggling students.

Beyond the Flipped Class

Why do we call it Flipped Class 101? Though we believe the flipped class is a viable method that has advantages over more traditional forms of instruction, we believe you can take the flipped class to the next level. We see teachers flip their classrooms for one or two years and then they move to deeper learning strategies, such as flipped-mastery, or a more project-based model. We do not categorize these as a flipped classroom, but as flipped learning. Flipped learning is the second iteration of the flipped classroom, where teachers move *beyond* the basic Flipped Class 101 model to more content-rich, inquiry-driven, and project-based classes. We completely document this transformation in our book *Flipped Learning: Gateway to Student Engagement* (Bergmann & Sams, 2014). In this book, we will share how these strategies work, specifically in the elementary classroom. For now, let's explore Flipped Class 101 a little more deeply.

Chapter 2

implementing flipped class 101

THOUGH THE FLIPPED CLASSROOM MODEL is a simple idea, it can be complex for teachers to implement. It sounds good to simply tell students to watch a video and then come to class to learn more deeply, but what if students do not watch the video? What if students do not have access to technology at home? What is a teacher to do then?

There are four major hurdles to flipping that you need to overcome. These are:

- Flipping Your Thinking

- Technological Barriers

- Finding the Time

- Training Students, Parents, and Yourself

Flipping Your Thinking

Flipping your thinking may be the *most* important hurdle to overcome. Why is this a big hurdle? Perhaps it is because many of us have been "doing school" the same way for many years and find change difficult.

Jon spent 19 years as a lecture/discussion teacher. That was a way he knew very well how to teach. In fact, he reached the point where if you told him the topic of the day, he could probably start teaching that topic without any notes, simply from his years of experience. In 2007, when we decided to begin using video as our primary means of direct instruction, Jon was the hesitant one. He didn't want to give up his lecture time, as he was a good lecturer (or at least he thought he was).

He liked being the center of attention, and enjoyed engaging in instruction a whole group of students. In his well-structured class, he liked being in control of all that was happening. When he flipped his class, he had to surrender control of the learning to his students. That was not easy, but it was the best thing he ever did in his entire teaching career.

Anyone born before the 1990s grew up in an information-scarce world. To access some information, we had to search through card catalogs and microfiche. Information was located in the schoolhouses, in textbooks and libraries, and in the heads of our teachers. Today, students can access virtually any information simply by using a device they most likely have in their pockets.

In light of this change, we must rethink how we teach our students. Consider any topic you currently teach, such as math multiplication, using a compass and protractor, creative writing, state history, or identifying the bones in the body. A quick search of YouTube reveals an array of videos available to explain these concepts. So the bigger question is this: How do we teach when our students already have access to an enormous amount of information? In this information-saturated world, the better question is: How do we teach them to filter and discern this valuable information?

Angela Boratko, a sixth and seventh grade math teacher in Connecticut, stated that both her students and their parents urged her to use a flipped curriculum. She adopted flipped learning to help meet those demands and to foster a better learning environment, stating, "Teaching my kids how to learn is more important than teaching them content." According to Angela, the flipped model works well with the culture of today's young students, as they look to the internet for most of their resources. Because of this, they are very comfortable going online for her video lectures. In fact, it is so natural that she knows that students in other classes seek out her videos. As a result of flipping her classroom, Angela says, her students learn more content than ever before.

Technological Barriers of the Flipped Classroom

In addition to his teaching career, Jon also worked as a lead technology facilitator at an elementary school. He and Aaron know that many educators have pigeonholed the flipped class model as only a technological solution to education. Much of the buzz about flipping has to do with using video as an instructional tool, which admittedly does involve a technological component. However, we disagree with those who see flipped learning as a technology-based educational practice. We see flipped learning as a pedagogical solution with an underlying technological component.

What, then, are the technological tools you need to master to flip your elementary classroom? Teachers often ask us, "What is the best tool to flip my class?" To this question we respond, "It is the one you will *actually* use." Our answer has a lot to do with you and your skills and needs. What type of a computer do you have? Do you have tablets? Do your students have devices? What is your comfort level with technology?

We know that there are a whole host of technological tools available for the elementary school teacher. Some are limited in features and are easy to use, while others are more complicated and offer more powerful features that add to the production value of your produced content. We understand that not all teachers are technology experts, so the tool you might use has a high degree of variability. We do see a few categories of technological tools that teachers must master to flip a class effectively, but before we discuss them, we should address a key question.

Who Should Make the Videos?

Should you make the flipped videos when there are already online videos on every conceivable topic? Without question, anything you teach has probably already been posted, but we believe that one of the hallmarks of a successful flipped classroom is the use of videos created by the teacher, or by a team of teachers at the local school. When we visit *struggling* flipped classrooms, we often see that the teacher is simply assigning video content created either commercially or by teachers outside their immediate network, rather than making their own. Conversely, when we walk into *successful* flipped classrooms, we usually find that the teacher is the video creator. We think the reason teacher-created videos are more successful is because they involve one of the fundamental features of good teaching: relationships between kids and their teacher! Some random person on the internet is *not* as familiar. Students recognize your investment in them through the content you provide. They see that someone who has direct involvement in their lives created custom content for them.

Despite the distinct advantages of using teacher-created videos, it is not absolutely critical to create your own videos to flip your classroom. If this is your first foray into flipping, or you don't have the time or technological skills to make a video, you should feel free to use videos other teachers and content experts have made. Although we know students really respond to the unique videos made specifically for them, we have met elementary school teachers who effectively use other videos, either as the primary source or as a supplement to their own.

Video Creation Tools

As of the writing of this book (bearing in mind that technology tools are always in flux), we continually observe five categories of video creation tools teachers are using to create flipped class videos: video cameras, document cameras, screencasting programs, tablet apps, and smart pens.

Video cameras. The easiest tool for most teachers to use is the camera built into their phone. Virtually all modern mobile phones have a video camera built in. Also, inexpensive handheld video cameras are capable of producing very high-quality video. A teacher could have someone (a colleague or student) use a camera or phone to record the teacher teaching a concept at a chalkboard. Students are even able to contribute to the shared learning by using their camera phones to make their own videos for class.

Document cameras. Teachers can use their document cameras to make flipped class videos. Many don't realize that this camera, which is designed to project an image in real time, can often also record video. When the document camera is hooked up to a computer (typically through a USB port), the software that came with the document camera often has the ability to record the screen. Therefore, the work a teacher performs under the document camera can be recorded, along with the teacher's voice. This method would work well in displaying a sentence diagram or annotating a primary document, for example. All of this is then converted into a video that can be shared with students.

Screencasting programs. These programs record whatever is happening on your computer screen along with audio, and in some cases, even a webcam shot. Screencasting is the number one choice for flipped class teachers to make videos. They typically create a lesson or presentation in some sort of presentation software, such as Microsoft PowerPoint, and use a screencasting program to record them teaching through their slide deck. There are even ways for the teacher to digitally write on the presentation so the students view the presentation, hear the teacher's voice, see a webcam of the teacher in the corner, and see whatever the teacher writes on the screen.

Tablet apps. Many apps for tablet devices can be used to make video recordings. Some popular apps include:

- Knowmia (www.knowmia.com): A comprehensive app that allows for simple screen recording and annotation. Free or Pro ($9.99 on iTunes).

- Explain Everything (www.morriscooke.com): A simple-to-use yet powerful video creation tool. $2.99 (iTunes and Google Play).

- Doceri (http://doceri.com): A tool that connects an iOS device to your computer, which allows the teacher to record their computer using the iPad. (Free or $30 on iTunes).

- Educreations (www.educreations.com): A simple web-based tool with a large following. Free or $8.25 per month subscription.

One advantage of tablet devices is that it is easy to write directly onto the presentation. For many of these apps you can upload a presentation to the tablet and then record the presentation. The tablet interface is an ideal choice when you need to annotate over pictures or want to have typical chalkboard features.

Smart Pens. There are a variety of smart pens available that will digitally record what you write on a piece of paper, as well as your voice. These recordings are then converted into video files (often called pencasts) and can be shared on the internet. Some of these pens require special paper, which may be purchased or printed online.

Hosting Videos

Once you finish creating a video, you must upload it to the internet for students to access. Many video hosting sites are available to do so. The easiest, and most familiar, to use is YouTube, assuming your school district does not block access to that site. YouTube is advantageous because the vast majority of students know how to access it, and their handheld device most certainly plays those videos. If you don't want to, or cannot, post to YouTube, other video hosting sites are available, such as Vimeo, TeacherTube, or Screencast.com. You can also post videos to the school website or to a learning management system (LMS).

Making Videos More Interactive

Once a flipped video is created and posted online, it is important to have students do more than simply watch the video. Video watching is a passive activity. Students are familiar with viewing Hollywood movies, where they simply sit and watch something designed to entertain. Watching an instructional video; however, is a very different activity, where students must come away with some level of understanding. We recommend that teachers build interactivity into the videos, which can be done in a variety of ways. You could have students simply take notes on the video, have them respond to an online forum, or use some other creative strategy. There are even software and web tools available that pause video at specified times and feature pop-ups of teacher-generated questions. Teachers then have access to user logs to identify who watched their video and how each student responded to its questions. Regardless of which tool is used, the key is to make sure students are actively engaged with the content and have something to do as they watch.

Making Flipped Videos Easy to Access

It is important to find an easy way to post video content, but it is equally (and maybe more) important to make it easy for students to access the videos. Learning management systems (LMS) are a category of websites that allow a teacher or entire school to organize digital content in one place. Students log in and interact with digital content in some way. An LMS can host videos, store online documents for students to view, and contain forums, blogs, and quizzes and assessment features. This software can be a one-stop shopping area for students to access all the materials needed for a particular class. Examples of learning management systems include Moodle, Blackboard, Canvas, Schoology, Edmodo, Haiku Learning, and My Big Campus, each with their advantages and disadvantages. Our recommendation is that schools adopt one institutional system so that students get all of their digital content from one site. Instead of using an LMS, some teachers have simply printed up a short notes sheet with a quick response (QR) code on the top. Scanning the QR code with a smartphone app leads students to their video, which they watch as they take notes directly on the paper handout.

We have recently noticed a new breed of LMS that is built around the concept of game-based learning, or gamification. Instead of students going to a site to access content and interact with it, there is a gaming component where students can unlock conditionally released options and quests. Once students have completed a quest, they can earn experience points or badges. Teachers connect with their students in a familiar way by using experience points and badges as an alternative way of reporting progress.

Of course, choosing the best LMS or game doesn't address all access issues. We are all aware of the technology challenges some students experience with homework, whether it be a lack of internet access or having no personal computer at home. Some of the issues of access seem to be decreasing, as many students now have personal electronic devices, even in economically depressed areas. Even so, some access challenges remain.

Some teachers and schools have creatively and strategically provided accommodations for those facing these barriers. We know of some who have offered support by opening up their classrooms for students over lunch or after school to complete their homework on school devices, while others help their students overcome these access issues by reserving some class time for them to watch the video assignments.

I Want Specific Tools

Writing a book that recommends specific tech tools is difficult because technology changes so quickly. If you are in search of just the right tool for you, we have created and placed resources on our website that feature several tools for video creation, hosting, and all things technological for the flipped classroom. You can find these videos at http://FlippedClass.com/tools. You can also scan the following QR code to reach this website.

FIGURE 2.1 A quick response code that leads to http://FlippedClass.com/tools.

Finding the Time

Time is an elusive commodity. Where can you find the time to create all these videos, post them on a website, build in interactivity, and re-create your classroom activities? We wish we had a magical answer to tell you how to find the time, but we don't. To be honest, successful flipped class teachers just make the time, and even more successful flipped teachers collaborate and work together to maximize their time. We carved out time before or after school when we committed to making this happen. We were seeing such positive results that we knew we had to do this for our students—that the extra work necessary to accomplish this task was worth it to us. Flipping your class will not make teaching easier, but it will make it better.

If your school or district leadership is supportive of the flipped classroom model, there are creative ways that can give you the time you will need to get started. The following are suggestions you and your school leadership might discuss:

- Hire substitute teachers for a day, while two teachers plan and create videos and in-class activities.

- Use professional learning team time to create shared video assets and other learning objects.

- Schedule common planning time for teachers.

- Use staff professional learning time to focus on flipping classes.

Training Students, Parents, and Yourself

The last hurdle to flipping a class is getting the appropriate training to implement the model well. There are three primary groups to consider for training: students, parents, and yourself.

Teach Students How to Watch Videos

A common mistake teachers make is assigning videos and assuming students will get out of the video what was intended, but this isn't always the case. Students need to know *how* to watch an instructional video. We have discovered that this is not something that comes naturally. Students need specific instructions on how to *interact* with the videos. We suggest you watch the first few videos in class with your students, while modeling how you want them to interact with it. Pause the video frequently and discuss how they should be listening, viewing, and thinking about the subject matter. Then, have students individually watch the next video in class while you supervise, ensuring they are appropriately engaging the video.

Keep in mind that not every student will master all the video content simply by viewing it. The point of the video is to introduce content so that students can master it *in class* with the real expert present—the teacher. We did this for an entire week with our high school students. We have heard from teachers of younger students that it can takes upwards of three weeks to teach their students how to interact with video content. The key is to know when your students are ready to interact with the flipped videos on their own, without your guidance, before assigning one.

Bring Parents Into the Conversation

The flipped classroom model can be confusing to parents, and it might need clarification. One approach that many teachers have used to accomplish this basic orientation is applying the flipped class model to their back-to-school night. They create a short video about class expectations that parents view prior to the back-to-school night. When face-to-face, the teacher and parents enter into a rich discussion of the flipped model and a deeper conversation about the nature of the class. Modeling a flipped class for parents is a highly effective way to introduce them to this new model, which is a huge paradigm shift for most parents. Instead of using video, other teachers send home letters explaining the model.

Irrespective of which method you use, communication is vital to your success. As a rule, you can never over-communicate with key stakeholders—especially parents. Todd Neslony, a Texas elementary school principal, who flipped his fifth grade class when he was a teacher, believes a flipped video made especially for parents is important in the primary grades. Flipping the instruction with the parents teaches them how flipping works in the classroom, in precisely the way their students will be learning.

Get the Training You Need

Flipping an elementary class is not just about assigning a video to be viewed at home, and then having students write a report or take a test during class. It is so much more. You must plan, engage, develop, and revise. We like to say that there is more than one way to flip a class. Each flipped classroom looks different, and it should.

Some teachers have given up on the flipped class when they discovered students didn't watch the video assigned as homework. Setting up a successful flipped class requires thought and planning. The best way to set yourself up for success is to network with other teachers who flip their classes, by attending a training session or conference on flipping, and, of course, by asking many questions.

Chapter 3

planning
for the
flipped classroom

WE ALL LEARNED HOW to plan a lesson, a
unit, or an entire class in our college education
courses. Many of these models for planning
lessons are effective, but when the flipped
classroom model is in place, many of these
frameworks need to be reexamined. Most
planning structures (and the teacher evaluation instruments) imply, or even explicitly
state, that there will be some sort of upfront
presentation of information to a whole class
of students. In a fully flipped classroom, the
direct instruction is at the individual level or
in small groups, so planning a flipped lesson
requires modifying the lesson planning and
delivery cycle.

The easiest adaptation to a lesson is to make a time shift, by moving the direct instruction out of the classroom space and putting the independent practice back into the class. Complex rearrangements of lesson elements are also possible in a flipped class. A simple shift in time and space allows teachers to implement the flipped model, even if they are working in an environment that does not allow much flexibility in lesson planning.

Let's break this down further by looking at how to organize a unit, a week, and a school day.

Flipping a Unit

How does planning a unit change when you implement a flipped model? In many ways, it is not necessary to change how you plan a unit. Delia Bush, a fifth grade math teacher in Michigan, teaches her unit on place value with the planning guide displayed in Figure 3.1 (see pages 30–31). In it, she has identified learning objectives, tied this to practice and hands-on activities, and created a video. We assume most math teachers already have a list of objectives similar to the ones in this chart. Most likely, these are already in place in most classes, with the exception of the video. So the only new component a teacher needs to develop is a flipped video.

One benefit of taking this approach is that it presses us, as teachers, to be very organized and intentional with content. The process of writing down objectives and creating or curating appropriate learning objects is a very powerful one. Teachers should implement this process, regardless of whether or not they flip. Thoughtful planning leads to thoughtful teaching, which is helpful to remember for those of us who often "fly by the seats of their pants." Before we flipped our classes, we often walked in and "taught" what we wanted, or just explained what was next in the curriculum. When we got serious about the flipped classroom, we realized we had to be much more organized about how we taught. This one exercise dramatically helped us think through what we were teaching, how it was taught, and what things we should stop teaching.

Learning Goal	Video
LG 1. I can read and write decimals to the thousandths.	2.1
LG 2. I can read and write numbers to the thousands.	2.2
LG 3. I can compare decimals to the thousandth.	2.3
LG 4. I can add decimals and whole numbers with and without regrouping.	2.4
LG 5. I can subtract decimals and whole numbers with and without regrouping	2.5
LG 6. I can use different mathematical properties to compute mental math.	2.6
LG 7. I can round decimals to the nearest whole number, tenth & hundredth.	2.7
LG 8. I can solve story problems involving adding and subtracting whole numbers and decimals.	2.8

FIGURE 3.1 Delia Bush's math unit guide on place value.

(Continued)

Watch-Summarize-Question	Required Homework Questions
What place value do you think would come after the thousandths place? Explain why you think that.	2-1 questions 2–22 (even only)
How are the numbers "one hundred two thousand" and "one hundred and two thousandths" different?	2-2 questions 1–5 & 14–21
Using the digits 1, 2, 3 and 4, what are the largest and smallest numbers you can make?	2-3 questions 16–27
Explain why Tyler has the wrong sum for this addition sentence and explain how to find the correct sum. 35.2 + 1.46 = 4.98	2-4 questions 4–6 2-5 questions 11–13
Write about a real world situation in which you would need to add or subtract decimals.	2-4 questions 7–9 2-6 questions 4–6
How can you use the Associative and Commutative Properties to help you mentally solve a problem?	2-7 questions 1–5, 7–8
Explain in words how you would round 10.239 to the nearest whole number.	2-8 questions 1–9
You get to take a turn at writing story problems. Story problems have 3 sentences: a statement (about the 1st number), a statement (about the 2nd number), and a question that needs to be solved. Your job is to write a story problem (using at least 3 complete sentences) that goes with any of the learning goals from this unit.	2-5 questions 14–15 2-6 questions 7–10

Flipping a Week

Once a unit has been planned, how would a teacher plan a week's corresponding classroom activities in the flipped model? In many ways, a teacher's planning cycle does not need to change too dramatically. If a teacher possesses a flipped video they have created or curated, they simply need to build in a few extra steps to ensure that students *interact* with the video, rather than just passively *watch* it. Here are a couple of suggestions on how to modify a typical weekly planning guide, with the flip in mind:

- **Give Extra Time and/or Advance Notice.** Don't assign a video on one night and expect all students will complete the homework. Students may need earlier notice. Some students are over-programmed and are on the go from the moment school ends. Trying to get some time in front of an internet-connected-device at the last minute may be a challenge for some students.

- **Allow Some Choice.** Not every student needs to watch every video. The key is not that they *watched* something, but rather that they *learned* something. For example, if there is an online game that teaches the same lesson, give students the choice to interact with that *instead* of watching a video.

An example of flipping a week can be seen in the sample lesson plan in Figure 3.2.

Unit Learning Goal	Day 1	Day 2	Day 3
LG 7 Rounding decimals to the nearest whole number, tenth and hundredth	Class: Active reading from math textbook HW: Watch Rounding Decimals video	Class: Rounding decimals worksheet HW: Re-watch Rounding Decimals video & summarize	Class: Discussion of video summaries HW: Explain in words how you would round 10.239 to the nearest whole number

FIGURE 3.2 Sample lesson plan or flipping a week, based on Delia Bush's math unit guide on place value.

Flipping a Day

Flipping a day in isolation, as a teaching strategy rather than a comprehensive approach to the classroom, can often be more difficult than flipping a whole unit or a class. This is because students are often not trained to operate within a flipped classroom setting. They must be prepared for a new way of completing the assignment.

Because many teachers' first entry point to the flipped classroom is to flip a few lessons, using a flipped lesson once every week or two, students need to be prepared for this new mode. The key to flipping a day is to have the lower-level cognitive content presented on the video, and an engaging activity planned during class time.

For example, using Delia Bush's unit on rounding decimals, flipping a day might look like the chart in Figure 3.3. With this model, the teacher is able to walk around the room and assist individuals and pairs of students during the 30-minute work time.

LG 7 **Rounding Decimals to the Nearest Whole Number, Tenth, and Hundredth (Day 1)**	Time: 50 min
Class discussion on homework: Rounding Decimals video	5 min
Active reading from math textbook: Section 2-7	10 min
Individual work on decimals problem set + pair work + check for understanding. Teacher walks around room assisting students.	30 min
Teacher clarifications and introduction of Day 2 Work	5 min

FIGURE 3.3 Sample flipping-a-day chart based on Delia Bush's math unit guide on decimals.

Traditional Resources

One of the misconceptions about the flipped class is that it is just learning through video. From the outside, it can appear that a flipped classroom is only about watching videos before class, and then doing other things during class time. Though most teachers start with this, they quickly realize that the real benefit of flipping the classroom is the opportunity to reinvent the class time. What happens in class is far more important than the video created and consumed.

Textbooks

Most schools still issue textbooks to students at the beginning of the year. Though many of these textbooks are now digital, they are textbooks nonetheless. We are not against textbooks—we see them as a valuable resource to help students learn. As a rule, flipped videos should not take the place of reading. However, it is important to be strategic about the textbook readings. You should keep assigning readings where appropriate, and use flipped videos where appropriate.

Other Readings

Clearly, textbooks should not be the only reading resource we provide to students. We want students to read other language arts texts, such as short stories, poetry, newspapers, web articles, and Twitter posts. Because some of these articles may contain unknown vocabulary or concepts, students may need to read the more complex content in class. In these cases, students would need an expert interpreter to help them understand the content in these higher-level articles. Media, beyond video, can also be used as an instructional tool. Students can read textbooks or online content, and then continue to learn in numerous other ways.

Angela Boratko, whom we met in the last chapter, created her own workbook that incorporated her flipped videos. In an effort to make the workbook interactive, Angela embedded within each lesson a QR code that links to her flipped video, and also includes prompts for students to demonstrate their learning (see Figure 3.4). These prompts require students to write out the video's learning goal, and then explain what they already know and what they learned as a result of watching the video. Then, the students must provide proof of this learning by solving a math problem and writing a reflection of the entire lesson. Angela's interactive math workbook enables her students to take a more active role in the learning process. Their interaction with the content is deeper and richer, and it encourages students to take more ownership of their learning.

Correcting Division Problems

Learning Goal:

What I Know:

What I Learned:

Proof: Check the division problems. Are the answers correct?

FIGURE 3.4 A typical page in Angela Boratko's interactive math workbook. Note the QR code, which links to the flipped video that corresponds to this lesson.

Many Flipped Learning teachers have become quite innovative with their reclaimed class time. The next chapter provides several elementary school examples of ways to engage students by altering class time.

Chapter 4

rethinking class time

THE FLIPPED CLASSROOM is not about the videos. Let's state this again: The flipped classroom is not about the videos! It is about how you re-envision class time. Since a flipped classroom frees up more time with students, the most important question to answer is, "What do I do with the recovered class time?" Ultimately, there is no "right" answer to that question, but it is necessary for teachers to begin the process of rethinking how their face-to-face class time is used with students. Many flipped learning teachers have become quite innovative with their reclaimed class time to help students develop a deeper understanding of the subject material.

Pre-teaching models have been around for well over two centuries (Thayer Method, inverted classroom, etc.). So are these flipping methods? We encourage educators to avoid semantic arguments about whether something is flipped or not, and focus on whether the needs of students are being met. There is little pedagogical difference between assigning a text to read, an activity to complete, a PowerPoint to click through, or a video to view. All of these methods are designed around the expectation that students will come to class prepared. Flipping the class with video is simply a way to reach a media-saturated culture with a familiar medium. There are other issues to consider when thinking about flipping a class.

Individualized Instruction

All of the strategies mentioned in this chapter can be included in the term "individualized instruction." Under a more traditional model of instruction, students receive instruction according to the preestablished pace of the class. In a flipped classroom, students get assistance with content right when they need it.

Managing the Chaos

One of the biggest struggles flipped class teachers face is choosing which students to help and when. This could be especially true in a classroom with student choice. Because teachers are constantly moving around the room assisting students, often the students who are the most demanding get the most help and attention. As you know, the most demanding students are not always the ones who need the most help. In a flipped class, we need to be cognizant of which students need more help, which ones are ready for the next challenge, and which ones have learned something incorrectly and need clarification. There are no easy ways to determine which students need the most assistance, as that changes from day to day and even moment to moment. Frankly, this is part of the art of teaching. The dance of the classroom is a difficult one, but it must be managed.

We had students come find us when they needed help, resulting in too many students standing in line and waiting for us. This affected how willing students were to seek us out. In identifying students in need, one strategy you might try is employing a visual cue. Cara Johnson, a teacher in Texas, uses a set of three colored plastic cups at each table to create a quick visual trigger to identify which students need help. A green cup indicates that students are fine and do not need any help; a yellow cup indicates the group has a question, but does not need an immediate answer; and a red cup indicates that the group of students are at an impasse and need immediate assistance. Using a system such as the cups helps students subtly indicate to their teacher their need of assistance, while giving the teacher a way to quickly identify individual and group needs.

Keeping Students Engaged

When Jon first started to flip his classes, he wanted to have several hands-on activities for his students to engage in during the class time. At first, he had students completing these activities almost every day. He soon realized that he was assigning *too many activities*. The pace for his students was too frantic, with students getting to the point where they were just trying to get through the activity, instead of really learning from them. What his students needed was more time to process what they had learned. There are times in the elementary classroom when teachers do the same thing. Worksheets are still commonplace in many classrooms, and they still can be useful for some students—however, making time in the classroom for simple activities that do not challenge the students to apply their knowledge may not be the best use of the class time. Homework for homework's sake is not a meaningful use of your students' time, or yours.

We have also seen the other extreme, where teachers have students watch a video and then complete worksheets in class, or answer simple lower-level questions, repeated day after day. Being able to identify characters or a simple plot structure, although beneficial to some, will not challenge them to think for themselves. Though students need time to process and practice, they also need engaging activities with which to interact. If the only change you make is the time in which you deliver direct instruction and worksheets, you have not made any pedagogical changes. You have merely made temporal changes, which will not help your students become more critical thinkers.

There are two ends of the spectrum where a teacher can err: either not giving students enough time to process, or giving them too much. We, as teachers, need to become more comfortable with silence, and to allow for time to think. This can be a challenge for students. Struggling is good for students and encourages them to find their own answers. Landing on either end of the spectrum can lead to disengaged students. Try to find a balance, giving students time for hands-on activities and enough time to process content with the expert teacher present. Realize that the sweet spot can change, depending on the day or even the class (see Figure 4.1).

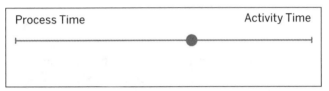

Process Time   Activity Time

FIGURE 4.1 The continuum spectrum. Note that the "sweet spot" can move depending on the subject. For example, math tends to have more process time, whereas science typically has more activity time in most elementary classrooms.

The key is to reinvent the class time. Flipping a class inherently provides a teacher with additional class time to involve students in more active learning.

Differentiation

One of the biggest problems teachers face in their class is the varying ability of their students. Some students are at a basic level and others are more advanced. In a conversation Jon recently had with his niece, Jesse

Petty, a second grade teacher in Idaho, she shared that this is her number one problem. At her Title I school, her students come from diverse backgrounds and need individualized attention.

Ultimately, flipped learning gives teachers like Jesse another vehicle for content delivery, which can be personalized for each student. Before we flipped our classes, we felt we were not very good at differentiation because we were tied to teaching a specific topic on a specific day. Once we moved the content delivery to be consumed by individual students, differentiation became easy and seamless. For us, flipped learning was the magic key to differentiation.

Flipped learning is a powerful tool for personalizing a student's instruction. Not every student needs to do every problem, write every sentence, or watch every video. Sheila Fisher, a third grade teacher in Georgia, assigns one video every other week for students to watch at home. Then, they independently watch two or three math videos each week in class. However, not all of her students watch every video. Students don't have to watch videos on content they already understand. Others who need a review will watch the videos multiple times. She believes that flipped learning is the key to her differentiation strategy. Each student is getting what they need, when they need it, and at an appropriate depth.

Note that you don't have to require that students watch the flipped videos at home. Many teachers simply have the flipped videos available in class for those students who need extra help and instruction, which allows for greater opportunities for differentiation. The idea of having the videos available in the class and not assigning them as homework is an idea called the In-Flip, which we discuss later in this chapter. Randy Brown, a Washington state third grade teacher, has created math mini-lessons for his students (http://bit.ly/mathminiflip). These mini-lessons are short videos on topics that students struggle with in his class. He organized the videos so that they are easy for students to find. When a student is struggling in a particular topic, such as finding the perimeter of an object, Randy assigns the perimeter video to that student. He realizes that some of his students need extra help, while others are ready for more advanced work.

You might be asking for more specific suggestions on how to use flipped learning to differentiate, but our advice for you is to just jump in and flip your class. Every teacher we have spoken to has realized that once they flip their class, differentiation flows naturally from the method. We recommend that you simply give it a try and see how much better you will be able to differentiate.

Choice

When we were traditional teachers, we simply taught our lessons to the whole group of students, on our timetable. They got all their information by attending class, and then went home and did homework. When we started flipping, our students received their information through video or some other way. This was better than the previous system, for many reasons, but there was still only one way to get information.

As we moved into our third year of flipping our classes, we realized that not all students learn best from any one method (lecture or video). We concluded that teaching through multiple modalities is the best way to organize a flipped classroom. We began to give students choices on how to learn new content. Some chose to learn by reading the textbook, while others liked learning through the videos, and still others wanted hands-on activities to learn. Instead of simply assigning one reading, video, or online simulation, we suggest you offer students a variety of options.

One particular student approached Jon and asked if he could skip the flipped videos and just read the textbook instead. The answer was clearly, yes! If a student can learn better by reading a textbook, there is no need for a teacher to require that student watch a video. If students learn better by reading, let them read. If they learn more effectively through online simulations, let them simulate. This may seem a bit disorganized and chaotic, but students naturally consume information in many different ways. Giving students a choice will ultimately help them be more engaged in the learning process.

Choice can be simple. Jon visited Cindy Gallagher, a third grade teacher at St. Celestine Elementary School, in metro Chicago, who had her students watch a video at home on determining volume. During class, Cindy spent about five minutes reviewing the content of the video, and then had her students complete three different classroom activities: a paper worksheet, an activity on their iPads, and an assignment to measure various rectangular objects scattered around her room. Students had to complete all three activities, but were allowed to do them in any order. Most students finished the activities in the order that the teacher presented; however,

Jon observed one student working in a different order. Jon asked him why he chose to go "out of order." The student proudly told him that since he was allowed to do them in any order he wanted, he was saving his favorite activity for last. This young student demonstrated that by making this simple choice, he was taking greater ownership of his learning.

Choice Boards

One way to implement choice into your flipped class is to create a choice board, like the one shown in Figure 4.2. (see page 50). These boards are set up so students cannot simply complete the easiest activities and avoid the harder ones. Instead, choice boards are arranged in a way that students must finish one knowledge-level activity, followed by an application-level activity, and concluding with an analysis-level activity. The choice board approach uses Bloom's taxonomy as a basis for determining levels of cognition.

Creating choice boards, and the corresponding activities, will take a considerable amount of time. We do not recommend that teachers who are new to the flipped class start with choice boards. Developing a library of videos and getting quality activities in class needs to be the first priority, but as a teacher moves along, choice can be a powerful addition to his/her class.

Activity	Knowledge/ Understanding- Level Activities	Application- Level Activities	Higher Order/ Hands-On Activities
1	Read textbook and take notes	Worksheet (Odd questions)	Interactive Activity A
2	Watch video, take notes, and interact with the video using online tools	Worksheet (Even questions)	Interactive Activity B
3	Search the learning objective online and summarize your findings	Interactive Online Simulation Meet with your teacher and explain the concepts	Student Project Design your own interactive activity that demonstrates the key point of this objective

FIGURE 4.2 An example of a choice board that gives students the freedom to choose the activity that most appeals to them.

Small Group Tutorials

Teachers often encounter several students struggling with the same content. The recovered class time from flipping a class allows teachers to engage them in small groups to review difficult concepts or clear up jointly held misconceptions. In these cases, teachers can bring those students together for a mini-tutorial at the whiteboard, and direct them as they solve the problems, while students who do not need assistance work independently. Teachers can also record these mini-help sessions, which would then give the students access to a video recording of the discussion for them to later review.

In our experience, students found this level of personalization very helpful, because they were able to have a video tutorial created just for them, custom-made to cover the difficult concepts *they* struggled with. These help session videos are also available for other students to access if they need also assistance with the same topic. Having a peer group working together on a topic they all struggle with helps students collectively understand and apply the math. The use of small group tutorials also allows for a more efficient use of the teacher's time by allowing him/her to help multiple students struggling with similar content.

In-Flip and Station Rotation

Some of the most dynamic activities used in the flipped classroom happen with the In-Flip, which is an adaptation of the station-rotation model of blended learning. A good explanation of the In-Flip is with the story of

Randy Brown, whom you met earlier in this chapter. He is an experienced elementary school teacher who has logged more than 30 years in the classroom. Throughout this time, he often struggled to meet the demands of his whole class while also giving struggling learners the attention they needed. After reading our first book, *Flip Your Classroom,* he realized flipping was just the resource he needed to duplicate his efforts and gain the class time he needed to reach all of his students.

Randy started making flipped videos for his students. But in his case, he had his students watch them in class. He divided students up, having half watch a video on personal devices and the other half work independently on the related material, with Randy's direct assistance. At some point during class, the groups rotated, giving the other half an opportunity to work with him, while the others watched the video. Randy's students were able to receive more direct interaction with him, especially the ones who most needed his help. As a result, his students' test scores rose. In time, Randy's station rotation method, with the flipped video being watched in class, became known as the "In-Flip." Randy went "all in" with his flipped learning, using it with multiple subjects through an In-Flip station rotation schedule, eventually creating more than 500 flipped videos.

Randy's In-Flip station rotation is based on two groups of students moving through a staggered series of stations (see Figure 4.3). The student groups are academically balanced so the higher achieving students can help the others. On a typical day, the stations would be focused on reading, writing, math, and art.

Round	Group 1	Group 2
1	Reading Page 1 Video	Art
2	Work on Reading/Writing Assignments	Reading Page 1 Video
3	Writing Page 1 Video	Work on Reading/Writing Assignments
4	Work on Writing Assignments	Writing Page 1 Video
5	Math Page 1 Video	Work on Writing Assignments
6	Work on Math Assignment	Math Page 1 Video
7	Art	Work on Math Assignment

FIGURE 4.3 Randy Brown's typical In-Flip station rotation for reading, writing, math, and art.

Randy begins a typical day by getting both groups started on an art project, which is generally related to the science curriculum. The art project takes multiple days to complete and is to be worked on during any extra time the students have throughout the day. Group 1 then transitions to the first round activity: watching a reading page In-Flip video. During this time, Randy helps group 2 with the art project. For the rest of the day, Randy moves back and forth between the two groups, helping where he is most needed, as the student groups rotate through the stations. If students finish a station assignment early, they have the art project on which to work.

The reading and writing videos and activities closely follow the required curriculum and his district's reading program. After watching the In-Flip video, the students work on reading and writing assignments. Ultimately, the students practice their writing and vocabulary by creating their own stories.

Randy has now been using the In-Flip for two years. Its biggest impact has been with the struggling students, with whom he now gets to spend quality class time. For example, two of his students are significantly behind the rest of the class. They aren't good readers, they never raise their hands in class to give answers, and they have difficulties keeping up with the curriculum. They are the type of students who fall through the cracks and often drop out of school. The In-Flip has allowed Randy to spend a lot of time with them, and they have become a couple of his favorite students. Instead of being on their own in their struggle, they meet with Randy every day, and he helps, mentors, and holds them accountable in their studies.

The In-Flip isn't just effective with the struggling student—the higher-achieving students are challenged more. Randy now expects a lot more from these students and has been known to send back student work that isn't perfect. He is able to differentiate in his instruction and to better provide challenge and help right at the student's ability level. Parents are happy that they are now able to help their child at home, and class visitors are simply amazed at the levels of student participation and engagement they observe.

Celeste Clemons, a Florida fourth grade teacher, is another educator who has embraced the use of stations. She uses them to teach math, creating classroom stations for peer review, math writing, math literacy, independent work, and a teacher station. Through all the stations, Celeste makes sure the students know they are "problem-solving," rather than "answer-getting."

In her class, each student group typically visits two stations a day. For the struggling students, their first stop is the teacher station, where they spend 20 to 30 minutes breaking down the math concepts for better understanding. Afterward, they move on to the peer review station, where they use small whiteboards to work on math problems from their workbooks, comparing their strategies and answers with the rest of their group. While Celeste models all the stations, she spends more time demonstrating for that group the activities of the peer review station. After Celeste has helped the struggling group at the peer review station, she freely moves about the classroom helping the rest of her students in other stations.

In another station, the math writing station, students do more than solve math problems—they engage in the practice of mathematical writing. There, the students learn how to write about math, still being accurate with the problem, and to understand how the problem applies to this mathematical practice. As they complete this assignment, they have to speak in math terms, using the proper math language. For example, the students learn, in both their speech and writing, to use the math term "product," instead of "answer."

Our final example of the In-Flip model is in the fourth grade elementary classroom of Texas teacher Ariel Pena. One of the reasons he uses the In-Flip is because most of his students do not have technology at home, so the videos must be watched at school. Ariel uses five math stations with five groups of students, one of which is a Spanish-speaking group. The groups move through a rotation schedule, which contains multiple approaches to studying math (see Figure 4.4).

Group 1	Group 2	Group 3	Group 4	Group 5
Teacher Station	E-Portfolio	IStation Math	Envision Vocab Activity	Flipped Class Manipul-atives
Flipped Class Manipul-atives	Teacher Station	E-Portfolio	IStation Math	Envision Vocab Activity
Envision Vocab Activity	Flipped Class Manipul-atives	Teacher Station	E-Portfolio	IStation Math
IStation Math	Envision Vocab Activity	Flipped Class Manipul-atives	Teacher Station	E-Portfolio
E-Portfolio	IStation Math	Envision Vocab Activity	Flipped Class Manipulat-ives	Teacher Station

FIGURE 4.4 Ariel Pena's math In-Flip station rotation schedule.

Before students divide into their groups, Ariel starts with guided math discussion with the whole class—where he delivers a 15-minute mental math mini-lesson on subjects like skip counting and place value. Students then move to their groups and the first station, based on the schedule. Most of the stations leverage technology, such as having students watch an In-Flip video, work with e-manipulatives, use adaptive assessment tools, use Edmodo to work on math problems, use a computer program to engage in math writing, and store their work in an e-portfolio. Students also have the opportunity to collaborate with the other group members at some of the stations, and they work directly with Ariel at the teacher station. The teacher station is where Ariel discusses the lesson and math vocabulary with students, and has them complete math exercises based on the content of the flipped video.

Although there are exceptions, our experience has shown us that In-Flip station rotation tends to be used more frequently in grades K–3, while a more standard flipped model where students view videos at home is more common in grades 4–6. Either way, having students rotate through stations located around the classroom is a good way to get students involved in a variety of activities while allowing for individualized teacher engagement. As we have shown, technology can be integrated within each of the stations to enhance student engagement and save the teacher time in class. One example—if students have access to digital devices, a QR code could be posted at each station, which would link to a short video explaining the objectives and directions of that particular station. With stations, there are few limitations for a teacher to make use of his/her instructional creativity.

Peer Tutoring

Although there is value in students wrestling with content independently, it is amazing to observe students helping each other learn. Students who have just learned something can often be better teachers than we are, simply because the learning process is so fresh in their minds. A novice who has just learned something new can provide meaningful insights to his or her peers about how to learn something new. Peer tutoring creates a collaborative atmosphere where students work together to understand a new concept, and it builds a sense of community. In many ways this mirrors the ad hoc study groups many of us organized in college, but it now happens in elementary classrooms, with the added benefit of the teacher being present to help the group when it reaches an impasse.

Australian teacher Matt Burns, who we met in Chapter 1, recalls one day watching two of his students helping each other learn math. The students shared headphones while watching one of his math videos. They would occasionally pause the video, explain it to each other, and debate what Matt was teaching. After pulling apart his lecture and coming to a mutual understanding, they moved on to the next lesson. Students are often the best teachers because they are closer to the learning and can explain what they have learned more effectively than a teacher. Peer tutoring has been around for a long time, but the interaction between Matt's students wouldn't have happened had it not been for flipped learning.

Another example of peer tutoring happens in the classroom of Randy Brown. Randy's class produces a news show called Room 21 TFK News, which they send in to the *TIME for Kids* magazine and news website (www.timeforkids.com). For these productions, Randy sets up a video camera and green screen in his class-room, and the students get to report on the news of their choosing. All the students get involved, each at their own level of ability, to record the show, edit the video, and add any necessary effects.

This activity allows for Randy to provide extra help to his students who need it, through peer tutoring. One peer tutoring mechanism Randy has incorporated is the "Five Tier Call Center Hotline." Most of the time this hotline is used for getting help with technical issues associated with the audio/visual aspects of Room 21 TFK News. The five-tiered system incorporates the following steps:

1. When a student gets stuck, he/she asks for help from a student in his/her small group.

2. If they are unable to help, he/she brings the issue to a designated leader of four other students.

3. If that leader is unable to help, he/she asks for help from one of four highly trained students in the class.

4. If none of those students are able to assist, there is one student who is the most proficient in the class, whose help can be requested.

5. Finally, Randy is available to help if the problem is beyond that top student's ability.

With this system, students are able to get the help they need from other students, and many have the chance to experience teaching their peers.

There are many decisions for a teacher to make before jumping into a flipped class model. In the next chapter we address key considerations for the younger learners in the elementary classroom, such as the best uses of video, getting parental involvement, and dealing with class absences.

Chapter 5

flipping
for **elementary**
students

OUR TEACHER EDUCATION PROGRAMS
have taught us that young children are in a
different growth stage than older ones, with
much of that research stemming from the
work of Jean Piaget. Piaget's theory of cognitive development states that 7- to 11-year-olds,
or preadolescents, are in the third stage, the
"concrete operational stage" (Ginsburg &
Opper, 1979). This means, simply stated, that
these students are concrete in their thinking
but are starting to incorporate logic and
inductive reasoning and problem solving.

This means that the abilities and educational needs of elementary students are different from the needs of middle- and high-school students, who are able to start thinking more abstractly. It should follow that a flipped elementary school classroom should look different from one in a secondary school.

According to a 2014 survey conducted by the Flipped Learning Network and Sophia Learning (http://tinyurl.com/pzll7lw), 80% of flipped teachers are in secondary schools, with only 15% being at the elementary school level. This may explain why there has traditionally been a lack of good resources for elementary teachers who want to flip. We know the sparse resources aren't due to a lack of interest. Our blog's most visited post is entitled, "Flipping the Elementary Classroom" (http://flippedclass.com/flipping-the-elementary-classroom), so we know elementary school teachers are interested in learning more. Otherwise, you wouldn't be reading this book! We hope this resource will help support you in flipping for our younger students.

In a recent blog post, Jon offered some basic advice to elementary teachers interested in flipping their class:

- Think of the flipped class as another technique in your arsenal.

- Start flipping around a lesson with which your students really struggle—and make a short video on it.

- Figure out where in the instructional cycle this video will be used.

- Keep the video shorter than 10 minutes—shorter for younger students. A guide might be 1–2 minutes per grade level.

- Figure out how your students will watch the video, and anticipate any access issues.

- Plan how you will check to see if the students have watched the video. Some have their students take notes or complete a web form.

- You might not assign the video as homework, but use the video as a center or station.

Beyond the creation and use of a video, there is clearly a lot to consider when planning a flipped lesson—such as deciding on the best subject to flip first. The previously described survey shows that 71% of all flipped teachers flip math or science classes, although there is recent growth in flipping in the humanities. Most of the elementary teachers we know got their start flipping a math class. If you are just getting started with flipping, we would recommend beginning with math and expanding to other subjects. Don't think you have to start by going "all in" and flipping all your subjects, even though some teachers do this. Some very experienced flipped teachers decide to only flip certain subjects. Just do what it takes to get started, and add to your repertoire as you gain experience and confidence with the flipped model.

Effective Uses of Video

Knowing what we do about elementary age students, what are the most effective uses of video for them? What is the proper amount of video for them? What kinds of videos will engage them? Although we have recommended some guidelines, it really is up to the teacher to best understand his/her students, and to design videos that work for them, making modifications when necessary.

Maryland fifth grade teacher David Dulberger first started using flipped video as a remedial tool in his math class. At that time, he had his instructional assistant watch the video in class with the struggling students, calling this "guided video watching." The instructional assistant helped students by rewatching with them the parts of the video that covered their areas of struggle, occasionally pausing it to have them practice their math and to check for comprehension.

In his second year of flipping his classes, David expanded his use of video to student-created content. He found the online educational resource Educreations (www.educreations.com), with which he had students create their own educational videos. David took the best videos and posted them for the other students to watch and to respond to with comments or questions. He also included other curated videos to provide them alternative math strategies, allowing the students to choose the ones that worked best for them. Eventually, students started becoming empowered to add their own external material into their assignments, telling David, "I hope it's OK that I found and used this other resource."

David also uses the videos to spark a class conversation. He will show a video in class of a current event, such as a SpaceX rocket launch, and then posts a related question. The student responses to that question serve as a discussion prompt, which promotes student engagement.

David uses an even mixture of original content and curated videos in his classes. He doesn't think you have to reinvent the wheel on every subject, but he generally believes that teacher-created videos are the best for students. When David does use curated videos for a lesson, he will still create his own introductory video. He also tries to find innovative ways to turn common everyday occurrences into flipped videos. For example, one time he was at a hardware store and recorded a video math problem on his phone in less than a minute. Another time, he recorded a video on potential versus kinetic energy while snowboarding.

For teachers thinking of flipping their classes, David recommends starting small and building routines— using one or two videos a week and making them directly related to the curriculum. Because students may need different resources, David thinks it is important to think through who will be watching the videos, and to target a group of students who might need a particular video. He also thinks it is helpful to build a fun routine into the videos to spice them up so that he can increase the engagement of students with learning.

Involving Parents

Anyone who has taught in an elementary school understands that parents have a big role in their child's education—more so than parents of students in secondary school. For most parents, flipped learning is likely a brand new approach to teaching and learning. Some parents may be interested and open to the model. Others may be uncomfortable, suspicious, or possibly even opposed to the idea. Most of the time, negative reactions are rooted in a fear of the unfamiliar. It is critical teachers understand this when they are preparing to flip a class. There will likely be a lot of education and communication necessary to gain the support and involvement of their students' parents.

We spoke with several elementary school teachers who have understood the need to involve parents in their flipping. One is Kris Szajner, a Minnesota Technology Integration Specialist who taught kindergarten for four years. He has involved parents by creating flipped lessons specifically for them. His flipped videos explain how the school system works, and offers suggestions on the best ways to help in their child's education. When he first started, Kris found that parent reception was initially shaky, but eventually improved once they understood what he was attempting to accomplish through flipping. The parents then embraced the model and consistently helped him.

Family engagement is crucial to make flipped learning work, according to Assistant Principal Kirsty Tonks and Jen Devaney, sixth grade teacher and project manager for Flipped Learning, both at the Shireland Collegiate Academy in the United Kingdom. To create this engagement, they present the flipped model at a school assembly at the beginning of the school year, and also send the students home with a descriptive leaflet to share with their families. They have found that educating and involving their students' families has resulted in more engagement at home. This also provides parents the confidence and increased ability to help in their child's education.

According to Celeste Clemons, her students' parents love the flipped classroom. To introduce flipping to them at the beginning of the school year, Celeste sends the parents a letter explaining the model. This letter also contains a link to her website, which provides more information about flipped learning and features a video of her explaining the nature, features, and benefits of the flipped classroom. In the parent letter, Celeste specifically addresses what the flipped classroom means for parents:

- Parents are able to be more involved in their child's math education.

- Parents have access to video content and are able to see how lessons are taught.

- Parents are able to have meaningful, content-related discussions with their child.

- Parents can encourage their child to take their time while watching videos, and remind them to rewatch, rewind, or pause, when necessary, to make sense of what is being taught.

- Parents can watch the videos with their child to help them review for tests.

- Parents are encouraged to bring any questions or concerns to the teacher's attention at any time.

Celeste concludes the letter by inviting the parents to meet with her to have any of their questions answered or to share with her their ideas for the flipped class. She reports that this early introduction to flipped learning has resulted in fewer negative phone calls and emails from parents.

Parental involvement is important enough that Jon wrote a blog post and dedicated an episode of his radio show to parents of students in a flipped classroom (http://bit.ly/ParentsFlip). In it, he lists his top five reasons parents should be thrilled that their child's teacher is flipping his/her class.

1. It will increase student–teacher interaction. Flipping provides more time for the teacher to connect individually with students.

2. It will help your child better understand the homework. Parents will also be able to watch the videos along with their child to see how the lesson is taught, better equipping them to help.

3. It will decrease your child's anxiety over homework. It is not difficult, and is often fun, for a student to watch a short video at home. The difficult work is done in the classroom with the teacher.

4. Your child will be able to pause and rewind his/her teacher. Students learn at different speeds, and teachers often talk too fast for good note taking and comprehension.

5. It will lead your child to deeper learning. Teachers of flipped classes often start engaging their students in more advanced activities, moving the instruction beyond test preparation or busy work. Their students often become actively engaged in dynamic class assignments, enthusiastically embrace the challenges, and learn to take responsibility for their own learning.

Dealing with Absences

Student and teacher absences are one of the biggest barriers to learning. When students miss class, they fall behind, which makes it difficult for them to catch up to the students who were present. We notice that elementary students are not just absent because of sickness—many are pulled out of class for various reasons such as IEPs, band, orchestra, or individual assistance. Many times, there are only a few students in class. Teacher absences can also be a problem, because it is often difficult to find a substitute teacher who can adequately replace the classroom teacher. Flipped learning solves the problem of both student and teacher absences.

When students miss class, they need an effective way to learn what they missed. The simplicity of flipped learning and its recorded lessons allows students to quickly and efficiently catch up on what they missed. Because the content is made available on the internet, many students come back to class from an absence ready to learn because they were still able to watch the video. Students who weren't able to watch it at home could even catch up by watching it in class.

When students are absent from a flipped class, they can more readily catch up because the direct instruction is still available. The flipped classroom helps to consistently deliver content to students, even when the teacher is absent. Too often a substitute teacher comes into the classroom without knowledge of the specific lesson, or an idea of how the assigned activities connect to the curriculum. Prepared videos allow students to receive the content the way their teacher desires, and the substitute teacher has a video resource to which to refer as he/she helps the students complete their assignments. For example, Angela Boratko's flipped interactive workbook proved helpful when she went on maternity leave. She was able to leave clear course expectations, a grading rubric, and interaction instructions for the workbook and the flipped videos. This ensured a smooth transition to the long-term substitute teacher who took over her class.

There are many examples of how elementary school teachers have flipped their classes, for a variety of subjects. The next two chapters will explore ways to flip elementary math, science, social studies, and English language arts.

Chapter 6

flipping math

AS WE WERE INTERVIEWING elementary teachers for this book, we discovered something very interesting. All of them started their flipped journey by flipping math. We believe that most elementary teachers start flipping math first because math is a more concrete, sequential subject. It also seems that in math there is a greater diversity of student ability levels than in any other subject. This chapter focuses on some ways that class time can be maximized to help students develop a deeper understanding of math. We will cover other subjects in the next chapter.

What should math teachers do with face-to-face class time? When you read about teaching math in the 21st century, you get the impression that you should be teaching through inquiry, projects, and simulations. We have talked with many experienced math teachers who have flipped their classes, and found that many of them feel guilty because their students spend the majority of the class time working individually or in small groups solving math problems. We want to assure you that having students solve problems in class is common practice and acceptable to most math teachers. Students need to practice to master concepts; however, we want to emphasize that you should also incorporate projects and simulations.

In Chapter 4, you read about how teacher Randy Brown uses In-Flip in his classes. He claims one of the best parts about this is his ability to conduct guided, and very targeted, practice sessions with students after they have just finished watching an instructional video. Once students watch a video, Randy has the students get out their whiteboards and markers. Then, he writes on the board the very same type of math problem the students observed in the video. This allows Randy to guide the class in practicing the very skills they just learned in the video. He is able to quickly see who understands the material, and who needs extra help. He is able to give and receive feedback instantaneously, right there in the classroom. Once he believes everyone has learned the material, the students can begin on their practice assignment.

We can paint this in broad strokes. Let's acknowledge that reinventing your face-to-face class time is an important component of flipping your class, that all students need practice in order to master math concepts, and that students should also have the opportunity to interact with projects or simulations. We want you to think of this as a continuum. At one end of the continuum a teacher uses class time for worksheets and practice, and on the other end you have students engaging in higher-order cognitive activities that challenge and enrich. Flipped class teachers who only use class time for practice are shortchanging their students. Teachers who only teach through projects don't often get through the required curriculum. A mix of both is needed. Many math teachers want to incorporate higher-order tasks for their students but have struggled to find the time to do so. Flipped Learning recuperates class time so that more of the higher-order cognitive tasks can take place in the classroom, with the content area expert in the room to assist students.

Guided and Independent Practice

Students have more time for guided and independent practice in a flipped class. Math teachers have traditionally sent students home to work on assigned problems. These problems are, in general, more cognitively complex than many students are ready to handle on their own. As a result, many students struggle to complete these tasks independently. This can be for a variety of reasons—for example, a student may have missed crucial content in class and simply can't do the homework. That student might then come to class frustrated, with incomplete work (or work copied from a friend) or with deeply rooted misconceptions. Without getting into the validity or value of homework, we propose that flipping your class can help alleviate some of the stress that homework can bring to a student. Simply flipping a class gives students the necessary time to work on problems in the presence of the teacher, which supports individualized learning, as teachers will then be able to spend considerably more time circulating around the classroom assisting students. This additional time for individualized assistance may be the single greatest benefit of a flipped classroom. By increasing both the quantity and value of the student–teacher time, more struggling students can have their needs met, while simultaneously allowing the high-achieving students to be challenged.

Students make many common mistakes when working on math problems. For example, when students add fractions of unlike denominators, many fail to first find the lowest common denominator. If this common mistake is repeatedly performed at home by students without immediate correction, incorrect math would be reinforced. However, if students make this mistake during class time, the teacher can quickly correct the student and reinforce proper math processes through supervised practice.

In flipping her math class, Utah sixth grade teacher Debbra Smith is able to effectively blend student independent work, small groups, and personalized guidance. She has organized and differentiated her class for students to work at their own pace. Debbra's goals include having students take ownership of their learning, as well as working together with their peers.

For their independent work, students watch her math videos and take notes using Cornell Notes. Students then can do that day's math activities alone or with a partner who is at their same level. Two or three times each day,

Debbra has her students work in small groups to practice their math skills, and sometimes in the workshops she has designed. For students who need help addressing a particular math deficiency, she uses the online educational resource MobyMax (www.mobymax.com).

Along with this independent work, flipping has given Debbra a lot of time for one-on-one meetings with students. She is able to connect with every student, every day, to review any math problem the student has missed. This allows her to ensure that each student receives individualized attention and the help he/she needs. Because of the activities flipping has supported, Debbra describes her math class as both more personal and more communal than ever before.

Math Manipulatives

Math teachers have been using manipulatives effectively for many years. Activities with manipulatives help students better understand and apply important math concepts by tactilely *manipulating* items that physically represent the abstract mathematical concepts. Whether those manipulatives are commercially made or created by the teacher or by students, they can effectively help students better understand difficult math concepts. One problem some math teachers face is the absence of enough class time to make full use of the power of manipulatives. Because the flipped classroom causes a drastic rethinking of how class time is used, manipulatives can be used more frequently.

Missy Northington, a sixth grade math teacher in Texas, flipped her class and uses the extra time with her students for activities, like creating factor label cards that students use to convert units of measurement into other units of measurement. If virtual tools are more your speed, there is a library of virtual manipulatives at Utah State University, with which students can interact online. The National Library of Virtual Manipulatives can be found at http://nlvm.usu.edu/en/nav/vlibrary.html.

Another example is Sheila Fisher's use of math manipulatives in her fifth grade math class, on finding the volume of an object. For this lesson, she has students watch and take notes on a video she made with her classroom document camera. She demonstrates on the video the formula for finding volume with cubes she snaps together, and counts their length, width, and height. Her students use a method of note taking called "WSQ (watch-summarize-question)," created by

California math teacher Crystal Kirch (http://flipping-withkirch.blogspot.com). Then they use their notes in small groups to discuss the video in class. Students who did not watch the video at home watch it in class during the WSQ small-group discussion. Sheila then has the students watch another video, hosted on Edmodo, and checks their comprehension by having them complete a Google Form (see Sheila's Google Form on volume: https://goo.gl/dlx9XB). Pairs of students then complete an in-class activity using manipulatives, building rectangular prisms using snap cubes and calculating their volumes. Finally, the students complete a final worksheet to check for understanding.

Interactive Simulations

There are many online simulations for students that can take the place of direct instruction. These simulations can be used as simple inquiry activities, where students explore mathematical concepts on their own, or for students to go deeper on a particular topic. These simulations typically engage students with graphs, geometric shapes, and other real-world applications of math concepts, allowing students to interact with virtual objects and learn from them. Students are able to explore key concepts simply by changing variables and discovering for themselves what would occur. These types of simulations are very useful and can take the place of direct instruction through flipped videos. Students can learn more deeply through discovery, rather than just interacting with videos on the same topic. Learning through these simulations can also be faster than some inquiry labs because of how efficiently students can manipulate variables in a virtual environment.

Following are some examples of online simulations and other resources that may be helpful for the flipped classroom:

- Geogebra (http://geogebra.org): Geogebra is not just for geometry. There are activities for all levels of math. Teacher-created lessons can also be viewed at http://tube.geogebra.org.

- PHET Interactive Simulations (http://phet. colorado.edu): A free resource, made by a team at the University of Colorado, providing manipulable math and science simulations.

- Explore Learning Gizmos (www.explorelearning. com): A subscription service with math and science simulations.

- Textbooks: Many textbooks also include simulations that directly tie into the content teachers may already be teaching.

Manipulatives and simulations are ideal, though not necessary, for teachers who have access to an interactive whiteboard. Small groups of students can gather around the interactive board and collaboratively experience these simulations together. Many of these simulations also have guided activities that may be valuable in helping students make sense of the content.

Challenge Problems

Missy Northington uses the recovered class time gained from Flipped Learning for increased differentiation and enrichment through challenge problems and puzzles. Missy uses Marcy Cook tile puzzles (www.marcycookmath.com), which are various math task manipulatives printed on cardstock, to give extra challenges to students who have demonstrated an understanding of the basic math concepts. Meanwhile, students who do not yet grasp the concepts continue to work on learning the math algorithms. These challenge puzzles promote complex problem solving, giving students a better sense of numbers and a deeper understanding of math. Although she has had these resources available to her for several years, Missy never used to have the time to use them. Flipping has given her that time, which allows her to continue teaching her students the foundational concepts of math, while keeping her advanced students engaged with fun and challenging math activities and providing them a richer math experience.

Although elementary teachers often get their start flipping math, flipped learning can be just as effective in other subjects. The next chapter provides examples of how teachers have flipped science, social studies, and English language arts to promote more classroom engagement and better student learning.

Chapter 7

flipping other subjects

ALTHOUGH MOST ELEMENTARY SCHOOL teachers start by flipping their math classes, flipped learning is not confined to teaching math. We spoke to several elementary school teachers who have flipped science, social studies, and English language arts. You can teach any subject in a flipped classroom.

Flipping Science

We began pioneering this instructional model in 2006 for our science classes. At first, our simplistic answer to the question about best use of face-to-face time was that we wanted our students to have more time to get our help on their assignments, and also to conduct more experiments. When we flipped our science classes, our students performed significantly better on their unit exams, and we were able to do 50% more labs (Bergmann & Sams, 2012).

Unfortunately, elementary school science is often not part of a student's everyday curriculum. Science classes tend to be taken periodically, reserving more time for subjects within the state standards tests. However, even with this limited time, flipped learning can still be a valuable way to provide science instruction.

Matt Burns uses the flipped model when teaching science. In one lesson on the environment, he poses the following question to his students: What can we do to improve our local environment? He and his teaching partner give the class access to 10 related videos they have made on the environment, on topics such as global warming and alternative energy. These videos serve as instructional resources for the students as they work in small groups during class. The students do not have to watch all the videos—only the ones they need to sufficiently answer the posed question.

In a lesson Matt teaches called "amazing adaptations," students focus on a specific animal or plant to explain an adaption it has made and why it is useful. To guide his students, Matt has created 10 high-quality videos for them to watch on different animal adaptations. Matt thinks it is important that he is a part of each video for his students, rather than simply sending students to outside resources like *National Geographic*. Although he will occasionally use curated videos, most of Matt's students tell him they prefer to watch the ones he has made.

Flipping the Lab

Have you ever been frustrated with your limited science class time and wished your students had more time to conduct experiments? Enter "Flipping the Lab." As teachers, we know students never have enough time to either do or finish experiments. Many teachers have shortened time for science, making it difficult to fit in lab instructions, lab investigations, and then lab analysis.

One way to deal with the time problem is to flip the lab instructions by creating a short video, which prepares students to start the experiment with little or no in-class direction from the teacher. To accomplish this, students watch a demonstration of the steps they will follow during the experiment, and then conduct the experiment in class. In the words of Ms. Frizzle from the Magic School Bus: *"Take* chances, make mistakes, and *get messy!"* Flipping science at the elementary level allows more time for experiments, so that students will not just hear about science, but will actually *do* science.

A slightly different take on flipping the lab can be found with Enoch Ng, a fifth grade teacher in Singapore. He has 38 kids in a class and still is able to conduct labs. He often has students design different experiments along the same theme, and then creates video summaries from each group. For example, his class was investigating factors that affect the rate of water evaporation. Some groups explored heat, others wind, others surface area, and others the amount of dissolved particles. Students conducted different experiments to test these effects in small groups. When they finished, Ng filmed quick summaries of each experiment for each of the different factors. He then edited these summaries into one video and required students to watch the summary video.

Although he did not have time or the resources for all his students to do all of the experiments, each of the students was required to know all of the factors that affected evaporation. This video was the key to making this requirement possible. Ng makes sure students explain not just what they did, but more importantly, how what they did led them to their conclusions. This is an excellent way to help students to think scientifically as they explain natural phenomena.

Flipping Social Studies

Like science, social studies is another subject often overlooked at the elementary level. In addition to his flipped science instruction, Matt Burns also uses flipped learning to teach history. As a teacher in Australia, much of his class focuses on his country's history. In his lesson on the Australian gold rush, Matt asks the class to identify the most significant event that occurred because of the gold rush. As a resource, he provides students a video to introduce 10 significant events that resulted from this moment in Australian history. The entire class surveys all 10 events and are then divided into groups that pick one event to explore more deeply. In choosing their event, each group is expected to research and argue why their choice was the most important one in following class presentations.

According to Matt, his videos are the launchpad for this assignment. Because his fifth graders have limited access to outside resources, he created many videos for this assignment. Even with their limitations, some of his students have incorporated books and outside videos into their work. Matt thinks it is important for students not just to understand history from a cursory view, but to have students go deeper by focusing on one topic. He has seen that giving students choices in their learning has created better student engagement and has allowed students to take more ownership of their own learning.

Skills Training

Students sometimes need help acquiring foundational skills that allow them to learn social studies material. In flipped classes, these skills can be demonstrated in a video that models techniques students will later practice in class with the teacher. A video shows the process or steps of a skill in a format that can be viewed and reviewed at a pace appropriate to the individual student.

Reading maps is one skill that is particularly important in social studies. One teacher we interviewed uses flipped methods to demonstrate the skill of map reading.

Before he flipped his classes, he found that students had difficulty understanding latitude and longitude. When he assigned homework to plot 10 coordinates on a map, he received multiple messages that evening from his students with questions about the assignment. He gave another lecture on the topic the next day, but still noticed students' blank faces, indicating their continued lack of understanding.

He decided to flip this assignment by recording and posting a seven-and-a-half minute video for students to review the material. Since they were able to pause and rewind the video during the difficult parts, the students gained a better grasp of latitude and longitude. After the video, he followed up with an in-class assignment to draw a map of the world, having groups of three or four students plot some assigned coordinates. He said the students had a blast with it. Once students started using the latitude and longitude grid to plot coordinates, its use and utility made sense to them, and their maps became more accurate.

Another important social studies skill is working with and analyzing a document. Some teachers have created videos that help students understand the differences between primary documents and textbooks, demonstrate strategies for reading history, and show students how to create outlines and analyze a document. To follow up their videos, students practice these skills by analyzing a document in class. Flipping has allowed teachers to differentiate their instruction to the varied abilities in their classes, and has enabled them to spend more time with the students in lower reading levels, which has proven especially beneficial.

Jon recently worked with a group of fourth grade teachers and observed how they used flipped learning to teach on the western U.S. expansion. These teachers had created a video that included a picture of a section of a historical text. In the video, one of the teachers discusses how to read a text like this, such as understanding why bolded words are important. The text is then analyzed through various lenses. For the lesson Jon observed, the text was read from the perspective of shopkeepers, railroad tycoons, Chinese rail workers, and settlers. In class the next day, on their own, students practiced the same skills shown on the video with the next section of the text.

First-Person Writing

One way for a student to become immersed in the course material is first-person writing, or writing from the perspective of a historical or contemporary figure. This allows a student to imagine a different context, move outside personal biases, and objectively analyze various situations.

One social studies teacher we know uses diaries and letters as first-person writing assignments. He has students create a diary as someone who was involved in the U.S. Civil War, which requires students to conduct historical research. In another assignment, students have to write a persuasive letter to the president, posing as a Delaware or Chickasaw Native American making a claim of fair or unfair treatment, and inquiring why they are being relocated to Kansas. Students are prepared for this assignment through a flipped video on the background on Native American tribes that were moved to Kansas, and about the relocation process along the "Trail of Tears," the route the displaced Native Americans traveled to their newly assigned lands.

Flipping English Language Arts

English language arts (ELA) is another popular subject for flipped learning. There is a lot of potential to flip ELA, with its emphasis on comprehension and skills training. Because reading and writing are important skills to have in all subjects, an effective flipped ELA class can benefit students across the entire curriculum.

Reading

In their reading instruction, many teachers are leveraging technology to help them flip their ELA classes. Three tech tools that have been used with great success are Curriculet (www.curriculet.com), Actively Learn (www.activelylearn.com), and Subtext (www.renaissance.com/products/subtext). These types of web-based programs allow teachers to freely use many works from the public domain, or to rent other titles, from entire books to individual poems. They can even upload their own. Teachers can embed within the text customizable questions, quizzes, notes, and media for students to engage in as they read them online. Students are also able to collaborate on assignments and shared activities.

These technologies often allow teachers to customize which extra material each student receives, personalized to his or her needs. The software tracks how each student engages with the site, such as which content is viewed and the length of time spent on it, as well as any responses to interactive content, making it difficult for a student to take shortcuts with the material. Most of these tools also feature dashboards that enable a teacher to view a student's progress through the activities.

Kris Szajner has embraced the use of technology in helping him teach reading and language arts. He often uses StoryBots (www.storybots.com), a web-based resource and suite of apps, and Have Fun Teaching (www.havefunteaching.com), a website with many teaching resources. Kris designs his lessons around commercially available video, which he embeds into Google Forms. His students then access these videos through Kris's classroom website. The Google Forms not only contain the lesson's video, but also feature questions for students to answer about it. According to Kris, Google Forms can also be configured to auto-grade the students' submissions.

In addition to external websites and programs, teachers can simply use a document camera with their recording software to model how to work with a reading selection. This method provides the students a model on how to start reading a text, and allows them to see the teacher's thought process as they are reading. Modeling what makes a good reader is a key element for students, allowing them to observe and transfer the process to their own work.

Writing

Under traditional teaching methods, writing is often assigned as homework. Limited class time is spent on the actual writing of book reports and essays, poems, and other writing prompts. By flipping the instructional method, students can practice the craft with the help of the teacher, and through collaboration with their peers.

According to Kirsty Tonks and Jen Devaney, at the Shireland Collegiate Academy in the U.K., the school has used a writing exercise that has looked at a variety of different authors to demonstrate how each uses language differently. One is children's book author Roger Hargreaves, who wrote the popular *Mr. Men* and *Little Miss* series in the 1970s and 1980s. In one assignment, students are given online access to a few of the *Mr. Men* books, with instructions to choose one to read before class. After some in-class activities centered on trying to understand the author's language choices, the students are tasked with writing their own books in class under the teacher's guidance. Once written, the teacher chooses one of the student books to put into a word cloud (www.wordle.net), and in class compares it to a word cloud from the text of one of the *Mr. Men* books.

Another writing activity at the Shireland Collegiate Academy is having students write a persuasive paper on the controversy over whether or not graffiti art is vandalism. On a public blog, the teacher posts some photos of graffiti art, some of which many would classify as vandalism. Students are to write about the posted photos in the blog comment section, which enables the teacher to assess his or her learning and thought processes. Other teachers at the school also write comments on the blog post, providing the students with good role models in how to appropriately and effectively communicate.

An extension of this activity is an in-class drama about graffiti and vandalism, featuring such characters as a park keeper, a street artist, and a woman whose wall has been vandalized. After practicing the drama in class, the students share their personal views with each other. The assignment culminates with the students writing a letter on behalf of a character in the drama, explaining how they have been affected by the graffiti.

According to Kirsty Tonks and Jen Devaney, students in primary school need a reason to write, and a real-world example on which to write. They state that students are also more open to digital writing than handwriting. They think this is because digital writing allows students to see their writing pieces as drafts that can be easily edited, not a final draft. They seem to be reluctant to edit their work after spending a long time writing it out by hand.

One of the best ways to help students improve their writing is to have individual conferences with them. However, with all of the standards that ELA teachers have to cover, it is hard to find time to meet with every student, much less manage the other students in the classroom during these individual meetings. Even after she flipped her classroom, high school ELA teacher April Gudenrath still struggled to find time to meet with every one of her 25 students on every piece of writing. So instead of giving up, she turned to video, wondering, why couldn't you have a flipped writer's workshop via video?

April uses a TechSmith product called Jing (www.techsmith.com/jing), which is screencasting software that allows her to record a video no longer than five minutes. The video is then saved and stored on her LMS, which she shares with her students through a link. Although five minutes may sound like a constriction, it allowed her to move into an editor role for her students' writing. April records her computer screen while a student paper is displayed. While recording, she highlights, manipulates the text, and explains the reasons editing suggestions are made. The one downside is that this is still asynchronous. In order to get more student involvement, she has them write a reflection on the feedback and share how they will incorporate the suggestions into their next revision.

Figure 7.1 is an example of the workflow of this style of writer's workshop.

Workflow	Time
Open and read paper on screen, make notes to share	5–8 minutes
Open screen recording software	<1 minute
Record screen while walking through changes/edits in paper	<5 minutes
Save file and share link with student	2–3 minutes

FIGURE 7.1 Writing conference workflow.

Did this make a difference? Her students say that it did. In fact, when they were interviewed for a video about April's classroom, she said her students pointed to this one event as what helped them become better writers.

Grammar and Spelling

Grammar and spelling are some other ELA areas that can be flipped. For many teachers, these are some of the easiest to flip, because they are skill-based. Flipping provides an opportunity for the independent practice that promotes foundational learning. Because it leverages the technology available to teachers, flipping grammar and spelling does not have to be difficult.

Grammar

There are several online resources available to help teach grammar. One commonly used resource is NoRedInk (www.noredink.com), an adaptive online resource that leads students at their own pace through grammar exercises on generationally relevant topics, incorporating immediate feedback and providing help with mistakes. Other frequently used online resources to help flip grammar are EDpuzzle (edpuzzle.com) and eduCanon (www.educanon.com).

One example of flipping grammar comes from Debbra Smith, who has students watch and take notes at home on a grammar video. This grammar video is not created by Debbra, but is posted on YouTube. It features a song and animation about idioms, which she claims the students really enjoy. To help them take notes on the video while they watch, the students use a Cornell Notes form, which Debbra has adapted for her assignments. The students are encouraged to bring their notes to the next day's class discussion, so they can reference what they learned.

After a short classroom discussion on idioms—for example, "raining cats and dogs"—the class starts an activity. Students are given a large piece of art paper to divide in half, with two good-sized areas on which to draw. Each student is given a unique idiom and is asked to use half of the paper to draw the literal meaning of the phrase. Once the students have completed their drawings, they are instructed to draw the figurative meaning of the phrase. If necessary, they are allowed to conduct online research about the meaning of the phrase. Once all of the drawings are completed, each student presents his/her artwork. For each student presentation, the class is given three chances to guess the figurative meaning of the phrase. If unsuccessful, the student explains to the class the meaning of the idiom. Finally, class concludes with a short discussion on how and why idioms are used. Debbra has found that by flipping her grammar instruction, she only has to perform a quick review of the content in class, leaving much more class time for students to engage in the grammar activity.

Spelling

Teachers David Dulberger and Matt Burns flip their spelling tests through the use of technology. David audio-records his spelling tests with Voice Recorder Pro and uploads the file to Google Drive. His students complete the spelling test asynchronously when they have time, and they have the ability to take it at home if they have missed class.

Like David's, Matt's 30-word spelling tests are recorded and completed online and can be taken anytime. His students have the ability to play back the test on their own devices and at their own pace. According to Matt, his students prefer this method of taking spelling tests to the traditional way. Recording the spelling test also enables Matt to differentiate more easily. For example, he creates three different tests for the three levels of spelling abilities among his students.

Another resource used by teachers to flip spelling is the online, game-based learning site VocabularySpellingCity (www.spellingcity.com), which also provides help in vocabulary, phonics, writing, and overall language arts.

As you may have recognized, no matter the subject, the idea of flipping remains the same. The key question of the flipped class is: What is the best use of face-to-face class time? This concept can even be extended to those classes outside the traditional "academic subjects" listed earlier. For example, Angela Boratko has observed her school's art teacher flipping how to use various art tools, such as a compass or an art knife. Because it is difficult for young children to sit through instructions, they can be delivered asynchronously to the individual learner. The students are then excited to get to art class to practice what they have learned. Instead of impatiently waiting through the instructions, the students get right to work on their art projects.

Angela uses flipping for her school's theatre productions, such as the musical, *The Sound of Music,* which she directed. For this production, she recorded video lectures for the students to take home and practice the music. This enabled Angela to spend much of their limited time together onstage rehearsing the finer points of performance, such as posture and projection, and to block the scenes. She even made separate videos for each character, as well as a few for the chorus, that students were able to use in preparation for their audition.

Each year, Doug Hinkle leads a theatre production of a Shakespeare play. Instead of needing the student actors to be together on stage to practice their lines, Doug flips this activity. He records the audio of the actors' lines and posts the audio files for the students to download. They are then able to listen and practice their lines along with the recorded ones.

As we have shown, virtually any subject can be taught in flipped learning. Once you have become confident in flipping your classroom, you may want to try a more advanced approach. The next chapter moves away from flipping specific subject matter to an exploration of the flipped-mastery model in the elementary classroom.

Chapter 8

flipped mastery

ONE OF THE GOALS OF EDUCATION is to encourage students to take ownership of their learning. This can be difficult through direct instruction and traditional teaching methods, which often promote collective instruction and moving students along to the next educational station without regard to the individual student's motivation and unique needs. Often with those methods, measuring true engagement and deep learning remains an elusive endeavor. This chapter explores how teachers can and do create learning environments where students are more engaged using the flipped-mastery model.

Although we addressed, in detail, the approach we call flipped-mastery in our first book, *Flip Your Classroom,* we thought we would dig a bit deeper into the topic as it pertains to elementary education. Mastery learning is not a new development in education, but was being developed in the middle of the 20th century by Benjamin Bloom, of Bloom's taxonomy fame. Essentially, mastery learning is a system in which learners are expected to demonstrate understanding, or "mastery," of a particular topic before moving through the rest of the course material.

In a flipped-mastery setting, students work through the course material at their own pace by accessing instructional video content, activities, simulations, and other learning objects, when they are ready for them. Operating in an asynchronous environment like this, rather than a synchronized environment based on a prescribed calendar, allows students the flexibility to learn at a pace that is appropriate to them. It has the added advantage that it can solve issues of access for students without sufficient technology at home. In a flipped-mastery classroom, video content can be easily accessed in class. Flipped-mastery is often the second iteration of a Flipped Class 101 that builds off of the video library a teacher has developed through the first phase of flipping his or her class.

Flipped-mastery places more control of learning into the hands of the students because it allows them the flexibility to create their own schedules of learning based around their own learning needs and styles. Some students may need some additional support and structure in a mastery environment. Providing them with daily, weekly, or monthly goals is one way to help students avoid getting behind. This system also allows high-achieving students to move more quickly through the course material, giving them time to work on independent projects of their own design.

Mastery in the Classroom

Angela Boratko incorporates mastery into her math class through a variety of learning objects based on a student's understanding of the material. Students work their way through three levels of comprehension: "Quick Quiz," "Think," and "Dig Deeper." During the 15- to 20-minute "Quick Quiz" stage, students work through math application problems. When they are finished with the quiz, they sit with Angela as she grades it. Those who earn below 85% on the quiz must continue to meet with her or their class peers until they gain the appropriate level of understanding. Those earning above that will move on to the next stage—the "Think" level. At this stage, students work on word and multi-step problems, which contain more visual interpretations and lattice methods. It is here where Angela also directs her students to an iPad math application.

Once students master those activities, they move up a level to "Dig Deeper." At this stage, the work is more tactile, problem solving is more collaborative, and the activities relate more to their campus community. One example at this stage is her assignment for students to leave the classroom to find polygons anywhere throughout their seven-building campus. After students bring back the items they have found, Angela has the students put the polygons together in a challenging way that is applicable to the real world.

Similarly, teacher Matt Burns also uses progressive steps in his class assignments. He calls it "Teach, Together, Try," and it is based on the gradual release model, "I do, we do, you do." For "Teach," students watch a video of Matt explaining a math concept. Students can then pause the video and attempt one math problem with Matt in the "Together" step. If they get the problem wrong, they must continue to watch the rest of the video. Finally, students are challenged to "Try" the math problem by themselves. Students only complete the assignment after they correctly answer 10 questions and demonstrate they have mastered the material.

Using Gamification for Mastery

Some teachers are incorporating gaming elements into their class instruction. In game-based learning, or gamification, students typically complete quests and other activities that allow them to "level up." Gamification often has rewards built in to help motivate students be more fully engaged in their learning.

One teacher who uses gamification in her math class is Debbra Smith, who has created games and game levels out of the required curriculum and textbook material. Each game contains a series of levels that need to be completed by a target date, which is explained in an assignment sheet. Debbra creates some videos and acquires others to go with each level, which students watch on their own or with a partner.

To complete a level, the student must take notes on the video and complete a worksheet, on which they must answer at least 80% of the math problems correctly. If they do this, the student is then free to move on to the next level. If a student scores below 80% on the math assignment, he/she meets with Debbra to discuss what went wrong and how to fix it.

Students are able to track their progress daily on game sheets posted on Debbra's classroom bulletin board. Students add a sticker "badge" next to their names each time they complete a level. This not only gives them a visual representation of their accomplishments, it also helps them identify classmates who are on their same level or have completed it. Then they know which students to partner up with or to seek help from if they need it.

According to Debbra, one important aspect of the game is for students to properly set goals for game completion. Although she uses a specific end date for the game as a broad guideline, students work with Debbra to individually set a unique deadline goal. Because each student's pace is different, she believes allowing the students to work at their own pace is critical to their success.

The game is over for the student once he/she has moved through all the levels, and completed a final check to prove he/she has mastered the material. Once students have completed the game, they meet with Debbra to discuss their work and the goals they had set, and identify whether changes need to happen in future games.

She then allows the students to ask her any outstanding questions before they take a post-game test. According to Debbra, most of those who have completed all their work score in the high 80% range and above.

Making the Jump to Flipped-Mastery

Jumping into flipped-mastery is a really big step. Many teachers flip their classes and never move to flipped-mastery. We want to emphatically state that moving from Flipped Class 101 to flipped-mastery was the best thing we ever did in our careers. It was very hard, but the level of learning and the degree to which our students took ownership of their learning was proof to us that it was the right decision.

To learn more about how to implement the flipped-mastery model, we encourage you to read the second half of our first book, *Flip Your Classroom,* and read *Flipped Learning,* which contains some teacher discussions about how they moved to flipped-mastery.

Flipping isn't a destination, but a transition from direct instruction to getting more creative in your class. It is an opportunity to change your teaching process.

Transitioning to projects is another advanced technique for teaching, but is a natural fit for the flipped classroom. The next chapter explains how projects and PBL can be successfully integrated into the flipped elementary classroom.

Chapter 9

projects

VARIOUS TYPES OF HANDS-ON ACTIVITIES can involve students in the learning process and allow them to explore their passions in the elementary classroom. Projects allow students to engage more deeply with content in ways that encourage creativity and understanding. They also give students the opportunity to work with different media, such as movies and art, and to use various skills that can motivate them to take more ownership of their learning.

Todd Neslony started assigning projects in his classes because he believed the students were too reliant on him for answers—asking him "thousands" of questions each class. In setting up his projects, Todd gives students very little instruction and allows students only a limited number of questions. An example of one of his math projects is on finding perimeter. In it, Todd prepares the students with a simple flipped video to watch at home, on finding the perimeter of a shape. The next day in class, the students divide into groups and trace the body of a member of their group. Then they are to find the perimeter of the tracing, converting it to three different units of measurement.

Todd provides the class various tools for the project: a meter stick, ruler, yarn, play dough, blocks, chart paper, and items with which to draw. He tells them they can use whichever ones they want to complete the task. Todd then walks around the classroom providing guidance and helping the students make choices. Along with his help, the students have to find their own resources, such as the internet, books, or peers, to figure out how to do the project. Even though this project challenges his students, Todd refuses to give them the answers or tell them what to do. He insists that they figure it out.

Todd's students learn to change the way they get the help they need. He has them working on projects nearly everyday—some small and basic, others more complex. Struggling students get pulled out of project time for remedial work, and others get placed in a project group with which he closely works. As time-consuming as this appears, Todd has been able to complete all the subject standards several months early, and has used the rest of the school year to review the material.

Another example is Missy Northington's project on proportions. On this topic, Missy starts with a traditional flipped approach, having students watch a video and practice the math problems. However, she allows them to take the quiz at their own pace. If the student finishes early enough and scores at least a 90% on the quiz, he/she moves on, choosing between working on the project or preparing for a full test. Missy states that 80% of the students choose to work on the project.

For this assignment, Missy employs PBL for students to demonstrate figuring proportions. She uses a project called "How Tall Is the Giant," adapted from a Creative Mathematics (www.creativemathematics.com) resource from educator and workshop presenter Paul Agranoff. This project provides students the measurement of a handprint left by a giant. The students have one class period to scale an item, with the correct proportion, to fit the giant's pocket.

Project-Based Learning (PBL)

Students can demonstrate their learning through other ways, such as through original and creative products. Creation is at the top of Bloom's taxonomy and enables students to demonstrate deep understanding and mastery. Many teachers think they are doing project-based learning (PBL) simply because they have their students working on projects. In reality, PBL is much more than this.

According to the Buck Institute for Education, PBL is a teaching method helping students gain knowledge and skills by working, for an extended period, investigating and responding to a complex question, problem, or challenge. As the former editor-in-chief at the Buck Institute, John Larmer, often says, "PBL is not dessert, it is the main course." Instead of projects being an add-on at the end of a unit, the project is the unit. The Buck Institute has been studying the efficacy of PBL for many years and has shown it to be an effective way to teach standards and content without driving the lesson with direct instruction, but using it when necessary (Buck Institute for Education, n.d.). Many teachers using flipped learning techniques have found that the extra time they gain allows them the flexibility to explore strategies such as PBL, while still maintaining a library of content that is delivered regularly, or as needed.

There are multiple approaches to implementing PBL in an elementary classroom, one of which is from Jang Jihyuk, a fifth grade teacher in Gwangju, South Korea. Jang first started flipping his class in a more traditional way, with videos before class and assignments in class. During a training on best practices in flipped learning, by the Korean nonprofit Future Schools (futureclass. net), he learned about PBL. Jang then took his students through a process in which they identified a variety of problems in their immediate geographic area. The students embraced the idea of project-based learning and collectively decided that they would better their community by designing and building a playground for the children in their community. This project was especially meaningful for these students because they were aware that one of the local playgrounds had been previously paved to use as a parking lot.

Jang devoted to this project about four hours of class time each week, for about six weeks. He used his regular math, history, art, and literature class time for the project, which he justifies because of the variety of tasks done by the students that were necessary to the project's success. Following are some examples of these tasks.

- Determine a location for the new playground (social sciences)

- Get approval from the appropriate authorities to build the project (social sciences)

- Design a playground where students would come (art, math, creativity)

- Learn and design safe playground equipment that meets local building codes (math, creativity, interacting with adults)

- Plot out the locations of the playground equipment around the playground (math, creativity)

- Locate funding to build their playground (not in most curricula)

The class even designed a special game that uses a Korean myth as its framework. This creative game connected what they had learned in their Korean literature to the playground and provided a fun way for students to engage in literature. They were even able to find an organization to fund the construction of their playground.

Jon had a chance to visit this class on the day they were reflecting about the steps necessary to make their playground idea become a reality. He was impressed at how the students had truly taken ownership of their own learning, and how proud they were of their project. Jang facilitated this ownership by guiding the students through a process of learning by doing something meaningful, for them and their community. As a result, their class had been transformed into a place of excitement, purpose, and engagement.

Student-Created Content

Once students understand the content, it is valuable to have them demonstrate it through the creation of their own instructional or explanatory material. One of the projects Todd Neslony assigns his students is to create a game board. Based on five questions for each of his state's math standards, students have to design all parts of a game—its rules, board, and game pieces. At the end of the project, the students trade their game boards and get to play each other's games, which the students really enjoy. Although he has had to help students create good questions that properly address the state standards, Todd views that process as a significant part of their learning.

Another example is in the classroom of Randy Brown. One of Randy's favorite class projects is the annual student-created puppet show. In Chapter 4, we learned about how Randy's class video productions are helpful for peer tutoring. In addition to those student news videos, each year the students create videos of the puppet shows they design. For them Randy lets his students create their own fun and silly scripts, and design and make puppets to match their story's characters. They record their narration and video record their puppet show in front of a green screen. Movie editing software is used to put together all of the elements to create a high-quality video production (see Figure 9.1). This project helps build collaborative learning and classroom engagement with even the most challenging students.

FIGURE 9.1 A screenshot of a scene from "Teen Titans," one of the student puppet shows created in Randy Brown's class. See a selection of full videos on his website (www.mrrbrown.org/puppetshows.htm).

Although Todd's and Randy's student-created content was made as part of projects assigned by the teacher, some students take their own initiative and start projects themselves. This is the case in the classroom of Celeste Clemons, where a group of her students decided, on their own, that they wanted to do an endangered animal project. After members of this secret group had completed their work during math time, they drew pictures of endangered animals and wrote about them—work the students kept completely hidden from Celeste. Celeste discovered their hidden project after reading one of the students' notebooks. When she asked about the animal project, the student told her, "We need to take ownership of our learning." She was so impressed that she joined their project and offered to help them. It then turned into a project for the entire class, with dedicated class time for students to work on related activities, including a student blog.

In another example from Celeste, a group of her students decided to start their own club, called the "teacher club." The club's members were students who had decided they wanted to be teachers when they grew up. These students went around the school collecting old teacher textbooks and worksheets, and pretended to be teachers. In response, Celeste set up some guidelines for the club's activities. Working within them, the students started to meet regularly outside of school—at a local fast food restaurant and in the park. The club members eventually offered to help other students at school become better learners. One even assisted with the after-school program. They were so dedicated to their class that at the end of the school year, the members brought home resources so they could create class worksheets over the summer months.

Celeste credits flipped learning for these two examples of student-initiated projects and content. These types of activities had never happened before she started flipping her classes. Now her students have more autonomy in their learning, and they no longer fear failure. Instead of just teaching, Celeste is now able to build a culture of learning in her classroom, where the students not only value their own learning more, they also care about the learning of others.

Flipped Mastery, gamification, and PBL are all advanced approaches to Flipped Learning designed to spark interest and challenge students to take ownership of their learning. Of course, these are not the only ways to promote student engagement. Flipped Learning will not look identical for every teacher and classroom, nor should it. Learning activities will vary, given the differences in each teacher's interests, skills, subjects taught, and experience with the flipped model, along with the varying needs of each class's unique student population.

Chapter 10

conclusion

SOME EDUCATORS HAVE ASKED us to provide a step-by-step guide to flipping their classrooms. Although this book serves to provide specific guidelines to elementary school teachers, these should be just that—guidelines. There is no one way to flip your class, nor should there be. Your flipped class needs to be customized and contextualized for each teacher's class and personal teaching style, as well as for the unique population at their school. The worst mistake you could make is to try to replicate everything in this book to flip your class. Instead, we want you to use this as a guide as you adopt practices that make the most sense in your context.

We had one goal in writing this—to move teachers away from the front of the room and encourage them to create active learning environments where *all students* are engaged in their own learning. A recent white paper entitled "Teaching for Rigor: A Call for a Critical Instructional Shift," from the Marzano Research Group, discussed what instructional strategies educators are actually using in classrooms (Marzano & Toth, 2014). Marzano and his group collected more than 2 million data points from the United States, finding that:

- 58% of all classroom time is being used for interacting with new content. The majority of this time is dedicated to direct instruction.

- 36% of classroom time is used for practicing and deepening content.

- 6% of classroom time is used for cognitively complex tasks involving generating and testing hypotheses.

These numbers need to change. The teaching of various subjects should not be just about learning the content about each. Students must be able to go deeper by asking, "Why?" They should be able to demonstrate relevant skills and apply their learning through creative, real-world demonstrations.

If you think we are being unrealistic about the real world of state tests, end-of-course exams, and high expectations, know that we still believe there is a place for direct instruction and content delivery. Students often don't know what they don't know, and elementary school teachers can help them through that discernment process. We have much to teach our students, but the reality is that many of us desire to do more application, more differentiation, and more projects. Yet, the tyranny of curriculum and the comfort of our old ways often keep us in a rut. We are seeing around the world that the flipped class is proving to be a way for elementary teachers to move toward more active forms of learning.

For instance, Doug Hinkle, whom you met earlier in this book, now in his 24th year in the teaching profession, started flipping his classes as a veteran teacher. At the urging of his interim principal, he got started after attending a workshop that featured a section on flipping. After visiting with us to learn more, Doug decided to adapt it to his classroom. His principal supplied him with some funds for the technology to start making videos, which he initially created for his math class. He later expanded his flipped videos with science, and eventually with social studies.

The school's limited technological infrastructure was an initial challenge, with its poor Wi-Fi signal and lack of devices for student use. This improved over time with the school implementing a "bring your own device" policy and boosting its wireless signal. Doug also found that the asynchronous nature of the flipped classroom allowed students to access the information anywhere and anytime, which virtually eliminated any access issues they previously had. This also helped solve the issue of content delivery for his many students missing class because they were traveling for hockey and soccer contests.

Doug claims he could never go back to the way he used to teach. Flipping his classroom has enabled him to give students more options and to personalize the learning and pace for each individual student, instead of his previous "shotgun" method. For students who need additional help on specific content material, he creates fine-tuned "short-shots" videos to target problem areas. Students who demonstrate they understand the material can move on, although they are always welcome to participate in a review, and the other students get the remediation they need. Flipping has also given Doug more opportunities to meet with each student and better get to know him/her. This has made him more aware of the gaps in his students' learning, and to fill them more effectively through this increased personal contact. It has also opened up opportunities for student leadership through peer tutoring.

Our challenge to you is to do what Doug has done. Find the parts of the flipped classroom model that work for you and merge it with the good teaching practices you have been doing for years, or wish you could be doing.

We encourage you to take these action steps to get started:

- **Take an honest look.** What percentage of your class time is involved in direct instruction or practice? Before we flipped our classes, our numbers were similar to the data from the Marzano Research Group. You may be in a similar situation. Think carefully about how flipping your class could help your students spend less time with new content and more time working on more challenging cognitive tasks.

- **Choose to begin.** Flip at least one lesson, or start by recording your live lessons for one year. What one lesson or topic do students in your class typically struggle with, one you find yourself repeating over and over? That is the perfect lesson to be your first flip.

- **Communicate.** The flipped classroom may be a new concept for students, parents, and administrators. Before you flip, develop an action plan to share reasons why you are flipping your class, and communicate your expectations to all those stakeholders.

- **Plan your flip.** It can be difficult to jump right into a fully flipped class or subject. It may be better for you to look carefully at your existing course materials, and spend some time planning how each lesson might (or might not) be adapted to accommodate video as an instructional tool.

- **Learn more.** This book is an introduction for elementary school teachers. Pick up a copy of *Flip Your Classroom* and the accompanying workbook. If you are intrigued by the flipped-mastery model, the second half of *Flip Your Classroom* focuses on how to implement it.

The world of information has dramatically changed since most of us were in school. We grew up in an information-scarce world where information resided in libraries, books, and the heads of our teachers. Today we live in a saturated world where information is easily accessible to anyone with an internet-ready device. Whatever elementary grade and subject you teach, there are now instructional videos on YouTube that teach everything in your curriculum.

If a YouTube video can replace us, we should be replaced! We realize this is a strong statement, but hear us out. Teachers are no longer the keepers of information, so our roles must change. We need to move away from being disseminators of content, and instead become facilitators of learning. As we embrace our new roles, we will be adding more value to our students' learning experiences. Instead of being replaced by a computer or a video, we are becoming more necessary and integral to education—because only teachers can help students explore topics more deeply, and only a content-area and learning expert can diagnose where students struggle. In a flipped classroom, the teacher is actually more necessary and more integral to the learning experience of all students. We are adding value beyond the content. We are ushering our students into an environment where they take ownership of their learning.

Will you embrace the flipped classroom? Will you take on the challenge of changing your practice?

references

Bergmann, J., & Sams, A. (2012). *Flip your classroom: Reach every student in every class every day.* Eugene, OR: ISTE/ASCD.

Bergmann, J., & Sams, A. (2014). *Flipped learning: Gateway to student engagement.* Eugene, OR: ISTE.

Bloom, B. S. (1968). Learning for mastery. *UCLA-CSEIP Evaluation Comment, 2,* 1–12.

Buck Institute for Education. (n.d.). *What is project based learning (PBL)?* Retrieved from http://bie.org/about/what_pbl

Ginsburg, H., & Opper, S. (1979). *Piaget's theory of intellectual development.* Upper Saddle River, NJ: Prentice Hall.

Marzano, R., & Toth, M. (2014, March). *Teaching for rigor.* Rep. Marzano Research Labs. Retrieved from www.marzanocenter.com/essentials/teaching-for-rigor-landing

Pink, D. H. (2009). *Drive: The surprising truth about what motivates us.* New York, NY: Riverhead Books.

References

Rosenwasser, D., & Stephen, J. (2014). *Writing analytically* (7th ed.). Stamford, CT: Cengage Learning.

TechSmith. (n.d.). Putting students at the center. Retrieved from www.techsmith.com/flipped-classroom-aaron-sams.html

Wiggins, G., & McTighe, J. (2005). *Understanding by design* (2nd ed.). Alexandria, VA: ASCD.